The Bliss Balance

The Bliss Balance

Create Success, Peace, and Happiness in Your Life

Rebekah Harkness

BIONIC
Press
www.bionicpressbooks.com

Cover design by Rebekah Harkness

FIRST EDITION

Published by BIONIC Press
Salt Lake City, UT 84088

Manufactured in the United States of America
ISBN: 978-0-9892448-2-4

To all humanity

Contents

Introduction

In the spirit of polarities and narrow-minded thinking, it has been argued that as human beings we either fall into one of two categories. We are either a spectator or we are a performer, and for whatever reason, we can't be both. I remember being introduced to this over simplistic approach to human psychology in middle school. At the time, it was refreshing to know that life was just that simple. All I had to do was figure out if I wanted to be on the sidelines or on the field. Being an athlete, that was a very easy answer. Duh, of course I wanted to be on the field. I wanted to be in the heart of the action. I wanted the glory, I wanted the sense of accomplishment, and I wanted to perform. In fact, I had pity for those on the sidelines. I couldn't relate to the idea of being a spectator. In my teenage mind, the spectators were missing out on all the fun, wasting their life away watching someone else experience life while they experienced nothing but solitude and boredom.

As I entered high school, I continued to be socialized in the value of being a performer. My coaches, parents, and teachers continued to echo the same messages. If I wanted to amount to anything in this world, I better be a performer. Performers are the doers. They make things happen whereas the spectators simply watch the performers do all the work. Even though it wasn't blatantly stated, it was clear to me that the most value was in being a performer. If I wanted to be happy, successful, and rich, I had no other choice but to perform.

Throughout high school, even though I recognized the over simplicity of this spectator/performer comparison, I still placed myself on the performer side. Not only was I socialized to believe that was the best side to be on, it was also my tendency - do, do, do, and do some more. Heaven forbid I be a spectator, no way. There was too much to do, too much to accomplish, and not enough time in the day to please and entertain all of my spectators. That is what performers do, right? My mind was constantly fixated on the next goal. I didn't even allow myself to enjoy the goal I had just accomplished. It was never good enough. Every feat I was going after was simply a means to an end, which turned into another beginning. There was no enjoyment in the moment; there honestly wasn't much satisfaction in any of it. I was plagued with anxiety, worry, and insecurity. The pressure to maintain a high level of performance all the time began to wear on me. I had high expectations of myself as well as high expectations from others. It was as if my entire identity as a human being solely rested on my accomplishments, and when I didn't perform to everyone's expectations, it was devastating. The smallest defeat would balloon into a catastrophe in my mind as the worry, anxiety, and fear of failure overcame my being. My entire self-worth was wrapped up in this violent marriage between unrealistic expectations, judgment, and fear of failure.

As the worry and anxiety began to paralyze me, my high level of performance became harder and harder to maintain. I felt myself slipping and losing the only identity that I thought existed for me. It felt as if I was watching everything that I had worked so hard for slip away and I had no control to stop it. The pressure, the judgment, the hyper-criticism, and other external stresses that I endured for so long had finally gotten the best of me, and all I could do was sit back and watch it unravel. Countless hours of study, countless hours of practice, years of dedication, and years of endurance had little to no value at this point. I had finally lost control. My mind and body were not doing what I was asking of them. In fact, it felt as if they were giving me the finger. After years of trying to overcompensate for a lack of control, a lack of safety, and a lack of unconditional love, I had reached my breaking point. It was years in the making, but the immediate problem was that I was nothing without achievement; I was nothing without a win; I was nothing without straight A's; I was nothing without success, and I was nothing without the ability to perform.

With the dissipation of the only identity that I had for myself, there wasn't much else to live for so unfortunately my only solution was to end it. It felt reasonable at the time. As a self-proclaimed performer not feeling in control of my level of performance, it felt as if I was living in a dark abyss with no identity. I didn't know who I was any more, I didn't understand why my mind and body weren't responding to my demands, and I didn't know where to go from there. I sure as hell wasn't going to be a spectator. I would rather be dead. Being a spectator at this point was insult to injury. With my tainted perspective, becoming a spectator just further accentuated the sense of failure that had already overcome my being. It was time to call it. I had made up my mind.

Luckily, I lacked resources, so my attempt to end my life was unsuccessful. I had failed at that too; one more bullet point to add to my failure resume. The day of my suicide attempt marked the beginning of a very long, lonely, difficult, and sometimes hard to understand journey of self discovery. Failing at trying to end my life, I begrudgingly gave living another shot. It was time to face my deeply rooted emotional wounds, adopt a new and constructive way of life, and reprogram my heart and mind. It was time for me to spend a little bit more time being a spectator and find value in that. It was time to put priority on the simple joys of life and let go of the internal pressure to perform. Just breathing was my main priority. At first, I didn't find much enjoyment in this spectator thing. In fact, it was hard not to feel even worse about myself. Clearly my belief system that I adopted as a child was not serving me very well. I remember telling myself that life shouldn't feel like this. Why did I always have to be performing and achieving and feel like a less-than? Why couldn't I just simply be? Why do I have to become someone in order to feel worthy of life?

Growing up, I was so caught up in being who everyone else wanted me to be. As a young adult, I didn't even really have a good sense of what I liked and what I enjoyed. As I was re-evaluating my existence and giving life another try, I made a list of all the things I was interested in and what gave me joy. I was desperate. I needed to be reminded of what felt good to me in this world and start from there. I was longing to experience moments of hope and happiness, even if they were brief. It was time for me to answer these three simple questions: What brings me joy? What do I enjoy doing? What makes me happy?

It was amazing at first how difficult it was for me to answer these questions. These ideas were foreign to the mindset that I developed for myself. Happiness? My life revolved around doing what "was right", winning, performing, and trying to be perfect. There wasn't much room for happiness. My entire self-worth revolved around my level of achievement. I didn't have time for this silly idea of happiness. I wasn't going to jeopardize my self-worth for something that I couldn't put on my resume. Duh! After much thought, I finally jotted some things down on my list: biking, Twinkies, star-gazing, and learning how to paraglide to name a few.

This list became my new to-do list. My focus

shifted from the need to achieve to the need to experience. I needed to remind myself what it felt like to simply do something without having a deadline and without striving for an end result. I bought a road bike and began biking. I would get up in the morning, hop on my bike and ride until my legs were like Jello. My daily routine consisted of biking, showering, and working. Repeat. I would sneak in a couple Twinkies every once in a while. Life was good. I was feeling alive again and excited to continue down my happiness to-do list. Paragliding was next. I was a bit nervous to take on the challenge of learning a new skill, but for whatever reason, I have always had a thing for flying. When I would drive past the flight park and see all of the paragliders and hang gliders in the air, I would feel a sense of excitement and peace all at the same time. I was drawn to it immediately. It resonated with my soul. I was determined to break out of my comfort zone and become a paraglider. This business of being happy was turning into a lot of fun.

I made some phone calls and signed up for the next paragliding training with a local instructor. It was thrilling! It felt amazing to get up early in the morning with the sun and make my way to the flight park to master this new skill. During the first week, I ran through the basics and began to conquer the feat of controlling the glider while on the ground. Towards the end of the week, it became time to take my first leap of faith. I had conquered the basics and was ready to jump off the mountainside and descend over 150 feet. I was anxious, but I felt so alive. When it was my turn to jump, my instructor attached a walkie-talkie to my harness so that we could be in constant communication while I was in the air. I established control of my glider, walked toward the end of the mountainside, and away I went. I was flying! It was better than I thought it would be. The sense of freedom and peace was amazing. I had found this so called joy that had been lacking in my life. Who would have thought that I would have found it in mid-air? I listened to my instructor's commands and slowly drifted back to reality. My first flight was a success. All of the students piled into the back of the SUV and headed back up the mountain. We were ready for round two.

Unfortunately, the only memory that I have of my second flight is waking up on the ground with blood gushing from my nose wondering what the hell happened and why people were yelling for a doctor. I lifted my head from the ground to try to catch a glimpse of my surroundings. I was dazed, confused, and nothing made sense, so I placed my head back on the ground and drifted off into never-never land. The next thing I knew, I was in the back of an ambulance on a very bumpy road. Pain surged through my body with every slight movement. I was begging the Emergency Medical Technician (EMT) for help. Being EMT certified I knew the drill. "Call your Medical Director now, so that you can give me some Morphine!" I barked. I didn't know I could be so bossy in a crisis. I don't even remember if they ended up giving me any pain relief or not. The next thing I do remember is being shoved into a helicopter to be transported to the nearest trauma one facility.

I had survived a mid-air collision with another paraglider in which I plummeted over 100 feet to the ground. My shattered pelvis was causing some severe internal bleeding, and I suffered open-compound fractures to both of my ankles. I was lucky to be alive. After the medical staff stabilized the internal bleeding, they had the daunting task of putting me back together. I was their modern day Humpty Dumpty. Wait a second, this wasn't on my happiness to-do list, what in the hell was I doing in the Emergency Room? I don't remember writing down anything related to being the next Humpty Dumpty. This had to be some cosmic misunderstanding. I didn't sign up for this.

My paragliding accident marked the beginning of another very long, lonely, difficult, and sometimes hard to understand journey of self discovery. Being stuck in the hospital for two weeks, and then stuck in bed for another three months was a performer's worst nightmare, and being told that my physical level of performance would never be the same just added salt to my wound. Again, my identity was shaken to the core. I had officially hit rock bottom.

At that moment, I had the task of making one of the most important decisions in my life. I had two choices. If I chose what was behind door number one, my life would revolve around self-pity, victimization, hopelessness, resentment, anger, and limitation. I had plenty of reasons to feel bad for myself. For one thing, the mid-air collision wasn't even my fault. I could spend the next three years of my life going after a financial compensation for the mental and physical anguish that this accident brought into my life. I could build an entire identity around my new disability and physical limitation, and I could be pissed at the world. Here I was, simply in search of finding joy again in my life and feeling like I was on my way, then…SPLAT! I literally had my face shoved in the ground. I couldn't help but ask myself if this was all a bad dream. Was this a joke? Is life really this cruel? Is God really this cruel? As I was contemplating what was behind door number one, it was a very tempting option to take, but I first had to consider what has behind door number two. If I chose door number two, my life would be propelled by hope, determination, positivity, transformation, rebirth, reconsideration, reprogramming, discovery, purpose, breakthrough, forgiveness, compassion, understanding, rethinking, and faith. At first, it was a bit daunting to think about the amount of effort it would take if I took that route. The path of least resistance was clearly door number one. That was a no-brainer, but as I looked deep within myself I knew which choice resonated with my soul. This was my opportunity to walk through door number two and focus on creating a life full of love, joy, happiness, and peace.

This devastating paragliding accident was one of the greatest gifts of my life. For the first time in my life, I was forced to be a spectator and given the opportunity to learn about and experience the value of observation and self-reflection. Being confined to a bed for three months, I spent a lot of time with myself. Because I was stripped of the performer identity that I had created for myself, I had to get to know the part of me that was left and previously ignored - the spectator. At the time, I had no idea of how much power and value was behind spectating and observation, but I was willing to explore it.

During this ordeal even though I had the support of family and friends, I knew that the only people that were going to get me through the challenge of rehabilitation were going to be me, myself, and I. Who would have thought that I would have to learn how to walk again at the age of 20? I had no idea how difficult it was going to be. Walking is easy, right? One foot in front of the other, repeat. Hah, it's kid's stuff! Well, it was quite the challenge. I hadn't used my legs in 12 weeks, my calves were the size of my forearms, and I had newly installed internal rods and screws in both of my ankles as well as a well-constructed chain of internal hardware holding my pelvis together. Putting one foot in front of the other wasn't as easy as it was 19 years earlier. I had found a new level of appreciation and gratitude for an ability that I completely took for granted. From that day forward, each step I took held meaning, and it still does today.

Over the next few years as I rebuilt my physical capabilities, I took the opportunity to rebuild and strengthen my emotional, cognitive, and mental capabilities as well. I utilized my fresh perspective of life, and I was bound and determined to better understand the art of spectating and observation. With my newly acquired physical limitations, I was forced to find a better balance of performing and spectating and better understand both sides of the coin. I had finally realized that being a performer in life didn't satisfy my soul and constantly left me wanting more, so I began to dissect and analyze what performing and spectating was really about. Performing is about driven behavior, reacting, logical reasoning and analysis related to cold hard facts. It is about taking in all of the immediate information and making a split-second decision while demonstrating determination and perseverance to achieve that end result. On the other hand, spectating is about observation, delayed reaction, considering the unseen when making decisions, thought, having faith, exercising compassion, paying attention to the feelings and sensations you have in relation to your experiences, expanding your perspective, contemplating, being mindful, and developing an understanding of how you fit in the universe.

As I moved forward, I held the belief that if I could maintain a balance between being a performer and being a spectator, then I would experience a happy, successful, and peaceful life. Over the next ten years, my belief proved to be right. Through much study and personal experience, I identified and compiled key components that will allow you to find what I like to call the bliss balance, which is just the right amount of spectating and performing in your daily life. There is a time to do and a time to be. Finding that balance will unlock the potential within yourself and allow you to live the life you have always imagined. Throughout this book, I have highlighted key thoughts, ideas, and behaviors that relate to spectating as well as performing. I have mapped out for you the perfect marriage of observation, faith, spirituality, knowledge, power, understanding, and ultimately action. I am confident that as you apply these principles and contemplate their essence, your level of success, happiness, peace, and bliss will increase in your life and in your soul.

The Bliss Balance

Part 1
Your Thoughts, Beliefs, and Mindset

You are what you think about whether you believe it or not. Thousands of thoughts pass through your mind each day. You consciously choose which ones to pay attention to, and thereby, shape your character. Some thoughts pass right on through without you even noticing, but some thoughts get stuck for minutes, sometimes hours, and sometimes days. You cling to and analyze them as your mental tape runs over and over and over. They are stuck until ultimately you decide to let them go. Day by day, you create beliefs around these thoughts that catch your attention and slowly your mindset is created.

Your mindset is a culmination of your thoughts, beliefs, habits, and feelings. It is composed of various conclusions and judgments that have shaped your perspective of yourself and everyone else. Once you form the foundation of your mindset, it begins to take on a life of its own. It becomes your default mode of operation. Unless you consciously interfere with it, it runs on autopilot and drives your behavior based on the instructions that you provided during its creation. This could be a really good thing or not so-good thing depending on the results you are getting in your life. If you aren't satisfied with the results in your life, including your level of happiness, peace, success, and prosperity, then it is time to consciously take control of your thoughts and change your mindset. It is critical that you focus on being a spectator of your thoughts. Be aware of them and remain emotionally unattached as you decide which thoughts you are going to devote your attention and which thoughts you are going to ignore. Don't react or make any quick decisions. It is important to simply observe your thoughts and then direct them to where YOU want them to go. This chapter focuses on broadening your awareness around how your thoughts are creating your reality and how to change your reality by consciously taking control of your thoughts. Your thoughts determine every outcome in your life. This is the starting line of your road to success, prosperity and bliss, so let's get started.

The Power of Your Thoughts and Beliefs

"Whatever the mind of man can conceive and believe it can achieve." Napoleon Hill

This is a pretty bold statement, so I would like to explain

the truth within this powerful message. Your thoughts and beliefs fuel your feelings and behavior. Your behavior then creates your habits, which in turn creates your reality and your belief system. Let me illustrate this principle with an example to clarify what this means. Let's say that you carry the belief that you are fat. Initially, your thoughts created this belief and now that the belief has been solidified in your mind, your mindset is going to automatically reinforce and look for evidence that supports this belief without any conscious effort. Perhaps, you might start to compare yourself to others to confirm that you are fatter than other people you know. Every time you look in the mirror you might say to yourself, "Geez, I am so incredibly fat!" All of your thoughts related to your body image reflect the belief that you are fat. Your thoughts feed off of each other and you remain stuck in this negative thought pattern. As a result, your feelings, actions, and habits have no other choice but to reinforce this belief and maintain this reality that you have created. If you were to maintain this belief and think the same thoughts associated with being fat, your life and reality would continue to reflect this "fake truth" that you created in your mind. The power of your thoughts is astronomical. You have the power and free will to choose whatever reality you want to live in. Unfortunately, as individuals we misuse this ability and imprison ourselves with these false negative thoughts and beliefs.

Take a minute and think about your life. Think about a belief that you hold about yourself, and think about how that belief has shaped your reality. Do you notice that you think thoughts that support this belief? How has this belief directed your thoughts? How have your thoughts affected your actions? How has this belief created your reality? I would really like to encourage you to do some self-exploration and really think about these things. The beauty about this process of how your beliefs and thoughts create your reality is that you can control it and manipulate it in your favor if you choose to do so. By paying more attention and better consciously controlling your thought patterns, you can create the reality that you really want.

Our beliefs that we hold, whether they are about the world, our environment, or ourselves, are simply thoughts that we have repeated over and over and over. Our thoughts create our beliefs through our observations, how we interpret those observations, and our imagination. As a result, if you want to change a belief that you have, you have no other choice than to change your thoughts. Let me illustrate this for you. Continuing the example that I just used, let's say that you carry the belief that you are fat. Let's first take a look at how this belief could have been created in the first place. This belief could have been created in a variety of different ways. Perhaps, you were teased as a child and labeled as fat. Maybe when you go shopping, you have a hard time finding clothes that fit, and you get discouraged and feel bad about yourself or maybe you went to the doctor's office for a routine physical and you were told that you were fat or overweight. Regardless, this belief was created by the repetitious thoughts surrounding previous experiences and the idea that you might be fat.

Remember your thoughts are going to automatically feed and reinforce the belief and thereby create and maintain that reality. Now in the spirit of changing this belief, let's say that you have decided that you are tired of being fat, and you want to improve your life. Well, the first and only place to start is with your thoughts. In order to change your reality, you have to change the belief. Now, you might be thinking to yourself, "How would I change my belief that I am fat if every morning I get up and look in the mirror and see a really fat overweight body?" To answer that, you can't face reality as it is and have reality change in any way. If you are going to simply observe your reality and think the same thoughts, you are stuck. You will continue to get what you have always got. Your brain doesn't have eyes. What we see is what we THINK we see.

You have two choices - you can either get up every morning, look in the mirror and observe your current reality and say to yourself,"Yep, I am fat...the proof is right in front of me." or you can get up every morning, look in the mirror and visualize the hot sexy body that you would like to have knowing that you are ready to incorporate some healthier habits and increase your level of exercise. The difference between these two choices is that in the first reaction, you are identifying with being fat. It is a part of your identity. In the second response, you are no longer identifying with it. You are now ready to identify with being healthy and taking care of your body. Once you de-identify with being fat, it creates some mental space for you to replace your old belief with a new and improved one. Keep this in mind as you start to identify negative self-destructive beliefs that you have and work on replacing them. If you can de-identify from your past thinking and identify with more positive beliefs, you will be well on your way to experiencing more success, love, and happiness in your life.

Using Affirmations

Your beliefs rule your life and determine your behavior - plain and simple. For example, if you have the belief that you speak well in front of people, then when the time comes, you deliver with confidence. If you have the belief that you don't speak well in front of people, then when the time comes, you get nervous and scared right off the bat, and as a result your performance suffers. If you believe that you will never get caught speeding, then you will often drive over the speed limit. On the other hand, if you worry that you will get caught speeding, then you stay under the speed limit. If you believe you aren't smart enough to start your own business, well, then you won't.

Think about your own life and think about how your beliefs shape your reality. Ask yourself how your beliefs are limiting your potential or keeping you stuck. Beliefs are powerful, so it is important to reflect on what beliefs are preventing you from reaching your dreams. Your success depends on your ability to change and eliminate your limiting and self-defeating beliefs.

A great way to change any self-defeating or limiting beliefs is through the use of affirmations. Previously, I mentioned that your beliefs are created by your thoughts. As a result, if you change your thoughts, then by default you change your beliefs. Affirmations help you do that. Affirmations are statements that describe a goal or state of being as already achieved. It is a form of auto-suggestion. By repeating affirmations on a daily basis, you begin the process of change. The change process begins as you invite the possibility of a different belief and a different reality. You repeat it over and over each day. You and your brain begin to accept the possibility of your affirmation as real. Your attitude begins to change; you begin to think of realistic approaches to bringing your affirmation into reality and incorporating it into your life.

Effective affirmations always start with the words "I am" and are stated positively in the present tense. For example, 'I am happy driving my 2013 black Mercedes Benz with chrome rims' is a good affirmation versus 'I am not happy with my current car'. The reason for this is because your subconscious mind thinks in pictures, so using the phrase 'I am not happy with my current car' causes your subconscious mind to focus on the picture of your current car and maintain your current reality. Be as specific as you can. The intent is to be able to visualize your affirmation and form a mental picture in your mind. What you need to understand is that your subconscious mind works with what you hold in your conscious mind. If you never bring in the idea or picture of owning a Mercedes Benz into your consciousness, then your subconscious has nothing to work with and you will never get it. Formulate some affirmations based on your goals and aspirations and repeat them to yourself in the morning and at night while visualizing them as you read them. This will allow your subconscious mind to start working for you and assist you on the road to your goals and dreams.

Planning Your Future

We get what we think about whether we want it or not. As a result of the powerful and irrefutable Law of Attraction, we draw to us the essence of whatever we are predominantly thinking about, and therefore our life experience reflects our predominant thoughts. If you are predominantly thinking about things that you want, your life will reflect that. On the same token, if you are predominantly thinking about things that you do NOT want, your life will also reflect those things. The important thing to understand is your thought patterns are much similar to a planning process. Your thoughts plan your future.

When you are appreciating, you are planning. When you are complaining, you are planning. When you are worrying, you are planning. Remember, you get what you think about whether you want it or not. Whatever your object of attention is regardless of whether you are appreciating it, fearing it, complaining about it, or wanting it, you are inviting into your life that very object of your attention and therefore planning your future.

When you worry, you are using your mind and imagination to create something that you do not want in your life. Worry is very counterproductive and paralyzing. When you worry, not only are you focusing all of your energy on something that you do not want, but you are also paralyzing yourself by negative emotions which in turn freezes up your mental capacity to solve problems. Having anxiety works the same way. When you are anxious, all of your energy is focused on something that hasn't even happened yet. Your attention is pulled from the present moment in to a future that doesn't even exist. Unfortunately, your focused attention on what you don't want is the very thing drawing it to you. The worry and anxiety is planning your future, and planning exactly what you don't want. It is important to be aware of this powerful phenomenon and actually use it to your advantage.

Take an active role in planning your future by starting with your thoughts and feelings. Get in the habit of feeling appreciative and grateful for the things that you love in your life. Gratitude has an amazing ability to multiply good things in your life. Appreciate all that you have and think about all of the goodness in your life. Set aside time every day think about all of the good things that happened during the day. It doesn't need to be a formal setting; the important piece is that you do it. Do it in the shower, while you are cooking dinner, or driving in the car. Be appreciative every day. On the flip side, be aware of when you worry or become anxious. Be aware of what you are complaining about. Actively turn your thoughts around and focus on positive, healthy thoughts. Remember, your current thoughts are planning your future. Make sure your thoughts are planning a future you want to be a part of.

Create a Success Mindset

In the beginning, you create your own mindset, and then ultimately, your mindset creates you. Your mindset, also known as your paradigm, is the sum total of your thoughts, habits, beliefs, values, opinions, and view of the world. It is the filter through which you interpret incoming information and the world around you. Your mindset shapes your life and draws to you results and outcomes that are the exact reflection of what your mindset expects. What you believe will happen, happens.

Because your mindset drives your behavior it is the ultimate cause behind the effects in your life. The results in your life are nothing but a reflection of what is going on in your mind. Examples of effects in your life include your income, your health, the level of satisfaction in your life, the amount of happiness, or your relationships. These effects are directly related to your mindset and thoughts – "A" (your thoughts) leads to "B" (your outcomes). It is a direct linear relationship.

Going back to what you learned in junior high about cause and effect, what happens when you try to change an effect without addressing the cause? Let me answer this one for you. The effect continues to occur because the cause hasn't changed. Even if you alter the effect, in the long run the original effect will resurface because the cause hasn't changed. Let me give you an example. Let's say that you attend a seminar held by a well-renowned motivational speaker. After the seminar, you are pumped. You are ready to change your life for the better, you are excited, and have a ton of motivation and energy. A couple weeks go by, your energy and motivation starts to lag and you begin to lose your enthusiasm, and slowly you get back into the same thoughts and habits that you operated on before you went to the seminar. The same thing happens with New Year Resolutions. In January, you are motivated, but then March rolls around and you probably can't even remember what your resolution was for the year.

Why does this happen to people with the best of intentions? Why is it that you can attend an inspiring seminar about how to change your life for the better, but you can't produce any results? It happens because you are trying to manipulate the effects in your life rather than addressing the cause. You were trying to change the result without changing your mindset. If you are focusing your attention on your outcomes, you have your attention in the wrong direction. Remember, your thoughts and mindset causes your outcomes. Because of this fact, it is critical that you focus your attention on your mindset in order to create long-lasting change in your life. The first necessary step is to take your attention off of any lack or limitation in your life right now, whether it is your bank account, job, house, relationship, or whatever. These things are only residuals of your past thinking. When you focus on what you already have in your life, you will create more of the same so take your attention off of what you don't want. Instead, put your attention on the things that you do want and pay attention to your thoughts related to these things.

As I have previously stated, your thoughts and beliefs determine your feelings and behavior. Your behavior then creates your habits, which in turn creates your reality. As a result of the law of attraction, it doesn't make any sense to put your energy and attention on things that you don't want, not even for a second. Energy flows where attention goes, and your thoughts manifest themselves in your reality. Because of this dynamic, it is incredibly important to focus on your successes in life instead of focusing on your failures. If you focus on your failures, you will continue to have more failure to focus on. If you want to be successful, then your goal should be to create a success mindset that you habitually operate.

Every memory and the essence of every experience are stored in your nervous system including your feelings, thoughts, and interpretations. Your brain uses these memories to form your beliefs about yourself and the world and uses your beliefs to mold your habits and reactionary thought patterns.

For example, if throughout your life you dwelled on your failures and allowed yourself to feel like a failure, your nervous system stores this mode of operation and creates a habit and thought pattern that creates more failure. Failure becomes your reactionary method of operation until you consciously make the effort to change it. Keep in mind, your brain and nervous system can't tell the difference between a real experience and an imagined experience. When you have a goal in mind and you use your imagination to visualize it and evoke feelings of having accomplished the goal, your nervous system and brain stores this information and activates your internal servo-mechanism to make it happen. Now something that you need to understand is that this can either work positively for you or negatively. On the positive side, you could have a goal in mind, visualize it, and evoke feelings of self-confidence, contentment, and success. On the other hand, you could have a goal in mind, visualize it, and evoke feelings of anxiety, worry, inadequacy, and failure. In either case, your nervous system and brain not only create a reactionary and habitual mode of operation based on your thoughts and feelings, but your thoughts and feelings become a determining factor of your results. The important thing to keep in mind is that you get what you focus your thoughts and energy on whether you want it or not.

Because of this phenomenon it is important that you recognize and be aware of those times you feel anxious, worrisome, or inadequate. Think about how often you experience these feelings. As you reflect on that, you should have a fairly good sense as to how much of your energy is focused on the possibility of failure rather than the expectation of success. If you want to create and experience success in your life consistently, it is necessary to form a reactionary and habitual mode of operation where you expect success every time and you automatically evoke the feeling of success.

In order to create this habit, there are a few things that you can do. First, you need to pay attention to your thoughts and feelings when you have a goal or task in mind. Visualize yourself accomplishing the goal or task with ease and focus on what you can control. Try to evoke feelings associated with the accomplishment. While you visualize, try to evoke the same feelings that would be present if you already accomplished it. Ask yourself,"How would I feel if I achieved this?" Picture it. Feel it. Focus all of your thoughts and energy on a successful outcome. Secondly, throughout the day, point out your successes to yourself, whether they be large or small. Immediately after you accomplish a task or goal throughout the day, acknowledge it. Tell yourself that you did an excellent job, evoke the feeling of success, and allow the nurturing of your self-confidence. The end of the day is a great time to acknowledge your successes. Right before you go to sleep, think about your victories for the day and remind yourself how good it felt to accomplish those tasks and goals. For those days that you have a hard time thinking of any successes during the day, relive and think about successes from the past and try to evoke those feelings associated with accomplishment. The important thing here is to focus your attention on your successes and create a habit out of feeling successful. What this does is it creates the habit of focusing your attention on what you want. I think it is safe to assume that you want success and you want to build on the success that you have already had. Success breeds success. When you are operating from a success mindset, you set yourself up for more and more success.

Your Mental Attitude

As human beings, we create an invisible fence surrounding ourselves with our thoughts, beliefs, and behavior. As the sole creator of your experience, this fence becomes visible through your mental attitude. Depending on how you build your fence, it will either limit your potential or it will allow you to expand into the person you were meant to be. Fear, self-doubt, negative thought patterns, and judgment create a poor mental attitude and results in a very tight fence around you. Self-confidence, faith, positive thought patterns, and awareness create a strong mental attitude and results in a fence that provides a lot of room for growth and success.

The type of fence that you build will shape your future and determine the quality of your results. As you think and dream, your life appears. If your dominant mental attitude is positive, peaceful, and loving, good things that share that same essence will surround you. If your mental attitude is negative, resentful, or bitter, bad things that share that same essence will surround you. Remember, we live in a universe built on the major premise of cause and effect. Every effect in your life has a cause, and your thoughts and mental attitude are the ultimate cause. As you think, you create your life. Your past thoughts have brought you to where you are today, and your thoughts today will take you to where you will be tomorrow.

Where are your thoughts and attitude taking you? You might not have control over other people or external circumstances in your life, but you have complete control over how you react to them. Strive to see the positive and strive to see your opportunity for growth in all things. All things, whether they are uplifting or destructive, await your acceptance, and as the master of your experience you choose which things you accept and entertain through your thoughts. If you accept defeat with a heavy heart and fearful attitude, you will remain in a state of failure. On the contrary, if you accept defeat with a willingness to learn and grow while choosing empowering thoughts, you will feel powerful and conquer your circumstances. It is your choice. No one can hinder you but yourself and the fence that you build through your mental attitude. Your thoughts mold your mental attitude and ultimately will act as a cause to every effect in your life. Harness the power that you hold within yourself and be the master creator that you were born to be.

In order to improve the current results of your life, you must change your thoughts and attitude. Do it one thought at a time. Pay attention to the invisible fence that you build around yourself as you entertain various thoughts, judgments, and beliefs. Build a healthy fence that promotes growth and success so that you give yourself the opportunity to grow into your own potential and make your dreams become a reality.

Your Words

I am sure you have heard the phrase, "Choose your words wisely." As human beings, one of our main forms of communication is through words. We use words to describe and depict the pictures that we hold in our mind. We don't think in words or phrases, but rather, we think in pictures and images. This holds true for both your conscious and subconscious mind. Words are what you use to verbalize the pictures or images in your head, and they are also very powerful in creating new pictures and images that you form in your head. Your mind automatically converts words into pictures, so your words are a very powerful tool in creating the reality that you want to experience.

Remember, your subconscious mind operates on the images and thoughts that you hold in your conscious mind. The images that you hold in your conscious mind are what your subconscious mind is compelled to bring forth. Your words play a big part in what pictures you paint in your mind throughout the day. When you speak, you are projecting images on the minds of others through your words, and when you listen, other people are projecting images on your mind. Let me illustrate this for you. Let's say that you are talking to a friend of yours and they say," I bought a new car last night." Automatically your mind begins to bring forth images of cars that you already hold in your mind, so you ask the follow up question, "What kind of car is it?" They answer, "It is a 2008 Range Rover Sport in black." At that point, your mind begins to narrow it down to the exact image assuming you have seen one before. If you haven't seen one before, other images of Sports Utility Vehicles come to mind.

Again, your mind thinks in pictures, so when it comes to your words, it is important that you understand how the words you use affects the pictures that are being painted in your mind. For example, let's pretend that you are faced with a challenge so you say to yourself,"I have a problem." The word "problem" automatically in your mind begins to create an image of something difficult and hard to solve, and your subconscious mind is activated to support that image. In the end, your statement ends up being validated and a part of your reality. On the other hand, in reaction to the same situation if you said to yourself, "This is a great opportunity for me to grow.", the word opportunity begins to create an image of something that has a huge upside and something that you can benefit from and learn from. Do you see the difference?

In order to be successful and live the life of your dreams, you must use words and phrases that support and create positive mental images. Your words are a direct extension of your thoughts. If you are ever wondering in what direction your thoughts are going, pay attention to your words. Your words are pure evidence of your thoughts. Choose your words wisely and keep in mind that your subconscious mind will turn your words into reality simply out of obedience. Use this power responsibly.

Mind Food

We live in a health-conscious world. Much attention, energy, and money is put into creating the mindset of making healthy choices when it comes to what we eat. We are constantly aware of and reminded of how many calories a certain food has or how healthy or unhealthy it is. There is a multi-billion dollar industry surrounding fad diets, successful exercise plans, or combinations of the two. We are told that we are what we eat, which is true, and on the same token, we are what we think, but my question for you is how much energy and focus do you put into what food you are feeding your mind? Do you put the same amount of energy into what you feed your mind as you spend counting calories, exercising, and watching what you eat?

The important thing to understand is that it is even more important to feed your mind with healthy "mind food" as it is to feed your body with healthy food. Mind food consists of anything that you put your attention on. This includes which books you read, television shows you watch, and music you listen to. And most importantly, it includes the thoughts are you nurturing in your mind. Your mind is a very sensitive instrument. The food that you feed your mind consists of the many things in your environment that influence your conscious and subconscious mind. It is probably safe to assume that at this point in the book, you now have the understanding that your thoughts create your actions, which in turn create your habits, which in turn create your attitude, personality, and ultimately your destiny. Who you are today is a direct result of your past thoughts and what you have fed your mind. The person you will be one year from now, or even 5 years from now, will be a direct reflection of the mental environment that you nurture in your mind today. As a result, the books you read, the television shows you watch, the music you listen to, how you spend your time, and what thoughts you nurture in your mind will determine where you are in the future and the level of success you experience.

I would like to encourage you to think about where

you want to be 5 years. Are the choices you are making today in line with where you want to go? Are you making conscious decisions about the type of food that you are feeding your mind? Are your thoughts nurturing the right type of environment for you to grow into who you want to be? Take some time to answer these questions. As fast paced as today's world is, you have so many opportunities to better utilize time out of the day and feed your mind with healthy positive thoughts that will catapult you on your journey to success and allow you to create the reality that you want. There are many times during the day where you can direct your thoughts on something else and still accomplish the task at hand. What I am referring to is the opportunity to use the time that is spent towards mundane daily tasks to focus your mind, visualize a specific goal, and direct your thoughts in a positive manner. For example, while you are driving in your car to work, instead of mindlessly listening to music, use that time to think about your goals, visualize the successes that you will experience throughout the day, or focus your mind on thinking positive thoughts about yourself. Use that time to feed and nurture your mind. While you are standing in a line or waiting for an appointment, focus your mind. Instead of watching television, read a self-improvement book. Remember, how you use your time each day will determine who you become tomorrow. Think about that and utilize the many opportunities in the day to feed your mind healthy, positive food.

The Voice Inside Your Head

Every single one of us has a voice inside our head. This voice talks to you endlessly casting judgment on yourself, others, and your surroundings. This voice is the collective programming that you have received since the day of your birth. It is the sum total of the beliefs, opinions, thoughts, and teachings of your parents, loved ones, community, and culture that you have been exposed to and coerced into accepting. What you need to understand is that this voice in your head is not you. Let me repeat, it is NOT who you are!

Now, you might be questioning whether this statement is true or not. To further validate my statement that the voice inside of your head is not you, let me ask you a question: If supposedly you are the voice inside your head, then who is the one doing the listening? Let me assure you, this voice isn't you. Your success and happiness in life will be contingent upon your ability to overcome and master this voice and regain your authenticity and power. Have you ever taken a moment and observed this voice in your head? Is it centered on love, kindness, and peace or are the underlying tones more of judgment, criticism, and rigidity? I am willing to bet that it is of the latter, and that's the challenge. The more you listen to this voice, the more it rules your life. Unfortunately, this voice doesn't have your best interest in mind. It is nothing more than a product of all the lies that exist in your world. This includes how you aren't good enough, how you aren't smart enough, how you will never make it, how things don't work out for you, and how life is full of lack and limitation. Don't buy into it. If you buy into it, you are sentencing yourself to a life of mediocrity and pain as you hand your life over to ignorant programming.

Transcend the lies and get on with your life. In the process of overcoming the voice in your head, the first step is to give yourself the opportunity to step back and observe the voice. Question it and seek to understand it. Think about where its ideas and beliefs could have possibly originated from and question the validity. For example, let's say that you are playing a game of basketball with your buddies and you miss an easy lay-up. Immediately following the miss the voice inside your head goes off and attacks you for missing such an easy shot. Perhaps it is saying, "You are an idiot! How could you miss such an easy shot? You suck!" Now before you buy into that garbage, take a mental timeout and become the observer, have some perspective and question the validity of the voice. Simply observe it. Notice the voice, but create some mental space from it. In the big scheme of things, missing a basketball shot isn't that big of a deal. Learn from it and keep trying. As soon as you have had a chance to step back and observe, ask yourself, "Where did this derogatory and judgmental pattern of thought originate from? Why would I allow this voice to talk to me like that? Who in my early life possibly taught me to be so judgmental towards myself? Did you get it from your parents, friends, family, or culture? Is that how your parents spoke to you as a child?"

Contemplate it and figure it out. Make a conscious

decision that you aren't going to buy into that negativity any more. Have more compassion toward yourself. Consciously refute the voice and tell yourself that it isn't appropriate for this voice to talk to like that. The more you consciously disagree with the voice the quicker it will be silenced. This voice inside your head should speak to you with love, patience, understanding, and kindness. If it is judgmental, derogatory, disrespectful, or mean, the blind programming that the voice is operating from is stealing your dreams minute by minute. Take the control back and learn to become the master of your inner voice.

Thoughts in a Day

According to experts, we have on average over 60,000 thoughts a day. This equates to about one thought per second assuming that you get about 7 hours of sleep. Experts also pointed out that of those 60,000 thoughts, 95% of them are the same thoughts that you had yesterday, and the day before, and the day before. That could either be a good thing or a really bad thing based on your thought patterns. No wonder why it is so hard to break habits. Because you have the power to control your thoughts, this fact alone demonstrates the power that you hold within yourself to create your own reality. Whether you believe it or not, you have the complete capability of controlling your thoughts and thereby controlling your destiny.

The beauty about it all is that once you consciously develop the habits of positive thinking and focus your attention on things you want versus things you don't want, your momentum will make things easier and easier. Because 95% of your thoughts are previous thoughts that you have already had your momentum builds each and every day. The downside is that habits that you have already created are harder to break. If you don't take the initiative to change your thoughts on a consistent basis and rewrite your internal program, then you will never achieve different results from what you have experienced so far in your life. Rewrite your internal programming and change the tune of the incessant, repetitive thoughts that are getting your attention throughout the day. If you are prone to seeing the negative, sabotaging your results, or isolating yourself, change your results by simply changing your thoughts. It takes your initiative and will to question and debunk your current thoughts and beliefs. In order to break the cycle, every time you have a negative thought, question it, reject it, and change it to a positive thought.

Because 95% of your thoughts are the same thoughts you thought the day before, it takes time to rewrite the program in your head that dictates the results that you experience in your life. You can't simply think good thoughts for a day and hope to change your life. It is about building a new way of thinking and a new way of life. It takes persistence and a strong will to change your life - one thought at a time. I guarantee that if you can exercise the persistence necessary to consciously reject every thought that you no longer want, you will begin to change your results and ultimately attain the success and happiness that you are longing for.

Who Are You Becoming?

At the beginning of every year, we tend to reflect on who we are and who we want to become. Usually, the health food and fitness industries cash in big time as we all make New Year's resolutions to lose weight or eat healthier. We all fixate on the idea of doing or changing a current behavior or habit overnight simply because it is the beginning of a new year. Unfortunately, by the time March rolls around the majority of us will give up on our New Year resolution and go back to our previous habit. Better luck next year, right?

Well, the fact is, it is extremely difficult to change a habit or behavior overnight and create a new habit that will actually stick. The reason why so many New Year resolutions fail is because we underestimate what it takes to truly become someone different than our current self. It takes work. You can't become until you have learned how to be – to be in the moment where you are physically and mentally. I am specifically referring to the importance of mentally and emotionally letting go of the past and not allowing yourself to feel negative emotions that derive from the past or the future. Guilt, shame, and low self esteem only exist because of thought patterns derived from your reaction to past events. Worry and anxiety only exist because of thought patterns focused on a potential future event that hasn't even happened and potentially won't happen.

If your focus and attention is tied up in your past, you are condemned to live in a world of your past. Your chance for growth and self-expression would be limited and stagnated. In order to give yourself an opportunity to become more than what you are, you must first get a better grip on mentally staying in the moment and letting go of your past. This takes a good amount of awareness, forgiveness, and discipline, but it allows you to gain some control over your mental faculties and create the necessary space for change within yourself. When you take a look at your daily thoughts, habits, tasks, and behaviors, who are you becoming? Remember, your present determines your future. Take a few minutes to really think about where your current thoughts and habits are taking you. Are the things you are doing on a daily basis getting you closer to who you are trying to become?

The present moment is your best asset, so use it to your advantage. Whether it is the beginning of a new year or you decide that it is time to change, instead of focusing on a specific action or behavior that you want to change, pay more attention to your thoughts and emotions. Recognize and be aware of those moments when you are overtaken by emotions derived from the past or future, namely guilt, shame, worry or anxiety. Give yourself some time to better develop your ability to be aware of and control your thoughts and emotions. When you feel yourself getting stuck in the past or mulling over past events, bring yourself back to the present. As you get better at this, your ability to succeed will be very much improved because you will have more power over your thoughts and emotions. You will give yourself the chance to become someone more than your current self.

<u>Self-Confidence: The Art of Believing in Yourself</u>

You have probably heard the phrase, "Regardless of whether you believe you can do something or not, you are right." The beliefs that you form about yourself play a huge role in either holding you back on the path of mediocrity or catapulting you forward on the road of success. You probably have a generic understanding of how important believing in yourself is, but the real question is how do you increase your level of self-confidence and change the beliefs that you hold about yourself so that you can obtain better results in your life? The first step in creating change in any aspect of your life, you must first do some self-reflection to determine where you stand. What are the current beliefs that you hold about yourself? This is a very important question to explore because it will give you a good idea of what dominant beliefs are driving your results. Whenever you have 10-15 minutes of quiet time, just start writing. Write all of the beliefs about yourself that come to mind. Simply answer the question, "What beliefs do I hold about myself?"

After you have a chance to let your mind go and write the beliefs that come to mind, read them back to yourself and make sure they resonate with how you feel. Once you have a final list, read through your beliefs about yourself and observe the amount of self-confidence that is either present or lacking based on your beliefs. I would be curious to know how many beliefs were positive and how many were negative. If you have more negative beliefs than positive that tells me your self-esteem has a bit of room to grow. I would really like to encourage you to spend some time contemplating and analyzing why you hold the beliefs that you do about yourself. These beliefs are driving the majority, if not all, of your habits and behavior. These beliefs are involved in determining the quality of your life, your level of happiness, and amount of prosperity you will experience. It is to your benefit to better understand these beliefs and change them if necessary.

As you self-reflect, think about where these beliefs originated from. Who helped plant the seeds of the beliefs in your mind? Researchers have determined that the majority of the beliefs that you hold about yourself came from your parents or caretakers. As children, kids see themselves through the eyes of the most significant people in their life. As a result, it is important to realize that the beliefs that you hold about yourself are merely the opinions of someone else until of course you accepted them as your own. Let me repeat, they are merely opinions - one perspective out of many.

After you identify your current self-beliefs, take a break and in a few days from now sit down and write the beliefs that you are choosing for yourself. Imagine the person who you intend to be and think about what beliefs this version of yourself would have. You are in control and have the power to choose what beliefs you will accept and what beliefs you will reject for yourself. Once you have decided what self-beliefs will help you become the person that you want to become, your next challenge is to change your current self-beliefs that are holding you back and replace them with these new ones. An effective way to do that is through affirmations, visualization, and auto-suggestion. Auto-suggestion is simply using repetition as a tool to reprogram your brain. In other words, you need to reprogram your brain and clean out the negative beliefs and replace them with new material. If you are really serious about changing your results, it will be necessary to take at least 15 minutes a day and go over the new beliefs that you would like to incorporate into your belief system. If you are consistent and do this on a daily basis for three months, you will notice that you feel a bit different about yourself. By default, your self-confidence will increase and as you focus more and more of your attention on these new beliefs about yourself they will begin to affect your actions, which in turn will affect your results.

The Power of Choice

The power of choice - it is a power you are born with regardless of who you are or where you live. It is a power that no one can take away. Regardless of your external surroundings you have the power to choose your perspective, your attitude, your thoughts, your mental and emotional outcome, and your direction. The power to choose is yours and only yours. You exercise your power to choose every minute of every day. You choose the thoughts you think, you choose your attitude and perspective, you choose your beliefs, activities, etc. In essence, you have chosen the life you are living now. Your life is simply a reflection of your past choices. Now, I realize the majority of you listening right now just got a little angry at me for suggesting that you have chosen your life, and I understand your frustration. If you are unhappy with your life you might be thinking, "If I really had the power to choose my own life, it would look very different."

The raw truth is that you do have that power, but perhaps somewhere along your journey you gave your power of choice away. Perhaps someone along the way tricked you into thinking that you are powerless or your life is chosen for you. It is a very easy trap to fall into. There were numerous times as a kid and a young adult where I felt powerless. I felt like my power was stripped and there was nothing I could do. I was tricked. But luckily, I found my way and regained my power by paying attention of the choices I was making with each thought, each action, and my perspective. If you are unhappy in your life for any reason, what that is telling me is that it is time to regain your personal power of choice and to take back any power you have given to someone else or to your circumstances.

There are so many challenges in life; it is very easy to surrender your power of choice to external circumstances, other people, and the world. Don't feel bad because people do it all the time. It is actually hard not to lose your power. Often times, individuals give up their personal power and allow circumstance to control their destiny, then they blame everyone else for their miserable existence. It is time to quit feeling so powerless and regain the power that you have always had. In every moment of every day, make choices that are in line with

30

who you are and who you want to be. Be aware of your thoughts. Consciously choose which thoughts you want to drive your behavior and actions. Make goals and exercise your power of choice to keep yourself in line with where you are trying to go.

Part 2
Spiritual Growth

Each one of us expresses and seeks spirituality in various different ways. Spirituality can be defined as a means of connecting with God however you want to interpret that. Some individuals experience spirituality through religious practices, others look to nature, meditation, prayer, religious text, writing, service, etc. Really the list is endless because it is up to each and every one of us how we expand our spiritual self, seek God, and figure out where we fit in the big scheme of things.

Life is all about growth and expansion. Regardless of whether you are religious or not, we are all seeking to become the best version of ourselves. Some individuals live from an established set of guidelines as determined by their religious affiliation and others define their own values and guidelines that shape who they become.

Either way, we are all moving towards the same outcome of self-improvement and a better quality of life.

Spiritual growth is another area that requires stillness, observation, and faith. It is important to be in spectator-mode as you expand your level of consciousness and awareness. Along with taking control of your thoughts, spiritual growth allows you to build the appropriate foundation necessary for taking correct action later. If you don't take the time to lay your mental foundation, you are setting yourself up to fail and never obtain the level of bliss, success, and peace that you were meant to enjoy. Without spirituality, your action loses value. It is important to find and embrace your true self, have faith, and find meaning in your life.

Your Mission: Growth

As human beings, our nature is to grow and expand. In fact, it is the nature of the entire universe and everything in it to expand and grow. There is a universal law that states,"If you're not growing you are dying." Nothing is stagnant. Sometimes you might feel like you aren't going anywhere, but the truth is you are - around and around in circles. There are endless examples of this universal law all around us. One example is flowers. They are either blooming to their utmost potential or wilting away and yielding back to the earth. Another example is the relationships in your life. As you nurture them, they grow. If you don't make time for them, they die.

There are countless examples of energy in motion,

but for you and your growth, it is important to understand that stagnation doesn't exist. Everything in your life is moving, so it is necessary to be aware of what direction things are moving. Always ask yourself, "Is it growing or dying?" If it is dying, figure out what you can do to change that. If you want to become "bigger" than you are and produce better results in your life, then you don't have any other choice but to grow. In becoming more than who you are today, you will come to understand that you grow the most in the midst of chaos while you are presented with challenges, hiccups, unforeseen stumbling blocks, and stress. When you are on the border of chaos and order and your back is up against the wall, you have only two options. Either you will experience a breakdown and get the same poor result and experience failure or you will experience a breakthrough, transcend your old-self, and increase the amount of success in your life.

Let me share an interesting illustration of this. In the process of winemaking, the grapes are intentionally stressed. They are grown in direct sunlight and not given very much water. The reason for this is because the grapes that pass the test and survive make the best wine while the rest collapse and die. The lesson here is that challenges, resistance, and chaos are beautiful things because they provide the playing ground for us to grow and "breakthrough" to that next level of personal growth. It is a scientific fact that we grow in direct proportion to our ability to sustain and withstand chaos. Embrace chaos and try to develop a welcoming attitude toward it because that chaos is sending you the message that this is your chance to breakthrough, become bigger than you are, and get that much closer to your goals and dreams.

The Power of Meditation

Meditation is the practice of quieting your mind and focusing your attention. It is the process of turning off the "noise", or habitual thought patterns, that are constantly going on in your mind. Meditation facilitates the opportunity to learn how to control your thoughts and attention. Your thoughts create your world, so meditation is a great tool that you can use to learn how to better control your thoughts and get a grip on the negative thought processes that are holding your back from success.

Meditation not only helps build your ability to focus, but it adds stillness and serenity to your life. Every day, you are bombarded with stimulation, whether it is at work, home or school. Television, radio, and the internet bombard you with stimulation and vibrationally demand your attention. You simply turn on the internet, and it is complete information overload. There are advertisements blinking at you, links in bold highlighting a picture, streaming video, or news blurbs attached to pictures appearing like a slide show. When you are in your car, you listen to music. When you are shopping, there is music playing. Even when you go to the bathroom at public establishments, more often than not there is music playing. If there isn't music, don't worry, you can pull out your cell phone and play games, text someone, listen to music, or surf the internet. Silence and stillness have become foreign and unfamiliar ideas, even to the point of uncomfortable. We have become somewhat dependent on a lot of stimulation. Silence has become awkward, and we feel restless if nothing is going on. How does silence affect you? Is it more comfortable for you to be watching television and reading the paper than it is for you to sit in silence by yourself for 20 minutes?

In order for you to fully reach your potential and tap into your unlimited supply of creativity, abundance, and health that is inside you, you have to be able to turn off the static and listen to the silence. If there is constant static, you are cutting off your source of intuition, creativity, and inner peace. Meditation is the perfect tool to keep that channel open. And not only that, but meditation has many other benefits as well including lowering stress levels and rejuvenating your mind and body. It has been documented extensively that 20 minutes of meditation is equivalent to 2 hours of sleep. Wow, talk about a trade off! Consider getting out of bed 20 minutes earlier and not only will you be giving yourself 2 hours of sleep, but you are training your mind to focus and make way for inner guidance.

Hopefully at this point I have peaked your interest and you are ready to give meditation a try. To get started, you will need to find a quiet place where you will be completely free from interruption. Start out by setting aside between 15-30 minutes a day for meditation. Once you find a quiet spot, close your eyes and begin by relaxing your entire body. You must be 100% comfortable. Once you relax your body, focus on your breathing. Breathe in and out. If you want, visualize the oxygen being transferred from your lungs to your blood vessels and traveling all through your body. As random thoughts enter your mind, acknowledge them and let go them go by continuing to focus on your breathing. If necessary as you focus on your breathing, count backwards from 25. With each breath, subtract one. Focus, focus, focus! It will be difficult at first because you must train your mind to focus. Your mind is used to jumping from one stimulus to the next. Once you build this new habit of meditation, not only will you find that focusing in your daily life is easier, but you will also be more in the present, feel more at peace, and get more done during the day. Your mind will also be open to new ideas and thoughts that will help you accomplish your goals.

As you begin to feel and see the benefits of meditation, you could use an internet search engine to research and learn more about it. There are many different meditation techniques and styles, so there is plenty of opportunity to mix it up, learn new meditation skills, and expand your ability to focus and find peace.

The Importance of Faith in Success

Faith is a key ingredient to your recipe for success. In fact, you won't get there without it. Many years ago, St. Paul defined faith as the substance of things hoped for and the evidence of things unseen. Faith gives you the opportunity to act as if you know. Meaning, you have full confidence in the knowledge that you have, and that knowledge allows you to cast out all doubt, fear, and insecurity. As a result, you press forward in action. When you doubt yourself, you act out of fear and apprehension. To further explain, faith is the process by which you use your thoughts and imagination to form images of things hoped for and of things unseen. These images that you create in your mind allow you to act as if you know. The point that I really want to drive home is that you are the one creating your own faith, to either work for you or against you. You create faith within yourself through the images that you hold in your mind, and the knowledge that stems from your faith is the means by which you are obliged to act.

As human beings, it is impossible for us to act against our inner knowledge, so it is extremely important that you use your faith to enlighten your path of success. For example, if you have the intention to live, you aren't going to step in front of a speeding car simply because you know that the car will kill you, and that knowing prevents you from stepping in front of that car. If you know or carry the belief that you don't have business savvy, you won't begin a business venture by yourself. If you know you are an efficient driver, you will drive fearlessly every day. Because you are in a state of knowing, no amount of persuasion can alter how you react to your inner knowledge. Referring to one of the above examples, no one is going to convince you to step in front of that speeding car because you know within yourself that it will kill you. That inner knowledge determines your action. Whether you realize it or not, you are always in a state of "acting as if you know". Unfortunately, sometimes what you "know" is holding you back from your goals and dreams. The good news is that you have the power to change the internal knowledge that you operate from, which will catapult you on the road of success and happiness.

Take a few minutes and think about what you have faith in. What images in your mind are shaping your reality and future? What internal knowledge have you created through faith? Ask yourself, "Do my images serve me?" Using faith appropriately is your key to success. Use your imagination and thoughts to create images of who you hope to be, what you hope to have, and where you hope to live. That is faith and you will by default act as if you know. Acting as if you know is a sure way to attain success. Use your faith wisely and effectively by holding images in your mind of where you are trying to go.

Faith vs. Hope

Faith is defined as being sure of what you hope for and certain of what you do not see. If you dissect this sentence, it is clear that faith and hope are two separate things, but in everyday life it is easy to confuse one for the other. As I have mentioned, faith plays a very important part on your road to success and on your quest for everyday happiness, so it is critical that you don't confuse it for hope. It is important that you don't accidentally identify hope as faith, because hope alone isn't going to get you anywhere. Faith and hope are quite different in their essence. Faith is driven by the power of knowing whereas hope is driven by the dilemma of not-knowing. Faith is single-pointed in its nature and its energy is concentrated in one direction and one outcome whereas hope is unsure of its nature, creates fear, and allows an acceptance that the outcome you are looking for might not occur. This lack of direction and concentration dissipates the energy and weakens the potential of your desired outcome.

Faith is what gets you off the couch. Faith allows you to harness your emotional energy in a focused direction and therefore increase your level of activity and purpose. There is the saying, "Faith without works is dead." To state that more accurately, works without faith is dead. Faith is the fuel that motivates you to do the work. Hope, on the other hand, doesn't even motivate you. Again, it goes back to knowing vs. not-knowing. Let me illustrate what I mean. If you are employed, five days a week, you get up and go to work. What do you think motivates you to do that? Could it be the fact that you know you will get paid, and therefore be able to financially take care of your family? Could it be the fact that you know that you are working your way up the corporate ladder? Could it be the fact that you know that this current position will allow you to gain the necessary skills and knowledge in order for you to start the business of your dreams? Do you see what I am getting at? You are probably operating on a great deal of faith every day and not even realizing it. Think about a time when you were operating from a mindset of hope. Did you have your fingers crossed that lady luck would deliver? I bet your anticipation paralyzed you. I can imagine you weren't very productive, perhaps felt a lack of direction, you weren't motivated, and as a result you didn't get the results you wanted. And why would you? Without a sense of knowing, it makes sense that you were reaping the spoiled fruits of self-doubt, fear, and lack of purpose.

Now that you know the difference between faith and hope, learn to recognize it in your everyday life. When you feel yourself operating from a position of not-knowing, sound off the alarms and do what is necessary to change your viewpoint to a position of knowing. The individuals that land the deals, make the sales, and bring home the bacon don't operate from a position of hope, but rather they operate from a position of faith. Have faith not hope, and I guarantee you develop faith in yourself and faith in your purpose, you will be well on your way to getting the results and the outcomes you want.

Ask and Ye Shall Receive

"Ask and ye shall receive" is one of the most common messages that you will find in a lot of new age/self-help books and in the Bible. It is a great message, but it can be very easily misunderstood. I would like to take a few minutes and clarify the intended message, so that you don't get lost in the idea that all you have to do to get what you want is to simply ask, and magically all of your dreams will come true. That would be pretty awesome, but that just isn't why we are here. We aren't meant to be mere consumers of the universe where we consume everything in our path and offer nothing in return. Life just doesn't work that way. Nothing in this universe is a "one-way street". Everything exists because of the push/pull, give and take, and the cause and effect relationships. There is always an interchange of information and energy, so the idea that you have in your mind of you sitting in your lazy boy and simply asking for success to show up at your doorstep needs to be altered a bit.

In truth, we live in a law abiding, compassionate, and loving universe. Whatever you ask for, you get. The catch is that often times you aren't aware of what you are truly asking for under the surface. If your energy is chaotic, worrisome, fearful, and anxious, your life and your results will reflect that same chaotic energy. If you constantly worry about money, talk about how much money you don't have, and feel jealous and envious towards people who have money, you will get exactly what you ask for......more lack. To better understand this concept; here is an example that illustrates exactly what I mean when it comes to asking and receiving. There was a woman that wanted to find a perfect mate, so she took a piece of paper and wrote down exactly what she wanted in a spouse. She was very specific and wrote down many qualities that she would like to find. Now, instead of just kicking back in her lazy boy and waiting for Mr. Right to magically show up in her life, she decided that she was going to take it a step further. She looked at her list of qualities and then asked herself the question, "What qualities would someone like this want in their partner?" She wrote her answer down as well. As she lived her day to day life, she embraced and emulated those qualities that her Mr. Right would probably be looking for in a spouse. Guess what happened? Mr. Right eventually showed up, and he had every quality that she was looking for. It was like magic. In essence, there is a lot of truth behind the phrase "Ask and ye shall receive", but remember asking involves your whole energy. This includes your thoughts, feelings, attitude, mood, intentions, words, and actions. You must align your whole being with what you would like to receive. And like magic, you get what you ask for every time.

Waves of Transformation

Life is meant to provide an experience that allows you to grow on every level. Life pushes you to be the best version of yourself and presents you with daily challenges and choices. One thing that you can count on and expect is that life will present you with opportunities to expand you consciousness. These opportunities are called waves of transformation. A wave of transformation can be defined as a period in your life or an event that requires you to change, expand, grow, exert more energy, or exhibit a higher level of understanding and consciousness. Can you think of an example of that from your own life?

When I look back on my life so far, I can easily pick out what I believe to be these "waves of transformation". Some of these waves were waves that I created through my own doing and my own destructive thoughts and habits and some of them were outside of my immediate control. Regardless, all of these "waves" gave me an opportunity. I had the opportunity to either use the experience to break out and expand my level of energy and consciousness or run the risk of allowing the experience to further shrink my true self and allow my ego to swallow me up and run my life. I am confident that if you were to take a few minutes to think about your life journey, you could identify your waves of transformation as well. In fact, I encourage you to do that right now and as you reminisce, ask yourself, "Did I ride the wave and end up on top or did I totally wipeout?"

Regardless of your past choices, don't be too hard on yourself, but rather move forward with this new insight. Know that waves of transformation are a part of life. You either create them yourself through your energy, thoughts, and habits or life simply hands them to you as opportunities to grow. Either way, I encourage you to welcome them. Ride the wave and learn the lesson that has been put before you. Now that you have this insight, you know the waves of transformation will be there so be prepared by welcoming the opportunity.

What Are You Chasing?

What is the true definition of success? I could ask 50 different people what success is and I would probably get close to 50 different answers. It is actually very interesting to hear people's responses. Some people view success as a lot of money, others, good health, good relationships, a good job, a nice house, freedom, having a family, some folks even get a bit daring and say that success is a combination of it all. It is interesting, especially in the American culture, success is a lot of times measured by the amount of money you have in the bank, the type of car you drive, your job, or the size of your house. It is often measured by external circumstances, but the ironic thing about it all is that psychologists and researchers have proven over and over again that status and external circumstances have nothing to do with the level of happiness that an individual feels on a daily basis, so the question remains, what is success? What is this lucid, mysterious, mystical thing called success that you would love to get your hands on?

Here is what nature has taught me about success. Nature very much illustrates the need to get out of "the chase". The chase is the idea that you alone are not enough and what you are is insufficient, so it is necessary to spend your whole life chasing after something that you think you need in order to be whole. People who are caught in the chase have the belief that they aren't going to feel happy until they reach their goal, whether it is more money, a bigger television, a nicer car, a bigger house, a better job, etc. Unfortunately, the reality of it is that the misery and unhappiness these folks feel on a day to day basis makes it just that much harder for their goal to manifest.

In order to better understand how to avoid getting caught up in the chase, let's discuss the life of a flower. A flower begins with a planted seed. The ground receives water from the rain; the water assists the flower in growing. The sun pitches in as well. The flower grows because that is its job. Its job is to simply be itself. It grows with no sense of urgency, no sense of time, and no sense of anything. Again, it simply is itself. It breaks ground, grows stronger and taller, and eventually blooms as a gorgeous creation. It has a unique gift to give to the world and its beauty reflects that uniqueness through being. It doesn't have to be anything else. There aren't any flower awards to win; there isn't a contest for beauty, speed, or size. It simply is. Any plant, tree, flower or even any animal reflects this powerful lesson. What more is there to do, but to be yourself?

Nature teaches us an excellent lesson in being and how to avoid getting caught up in the chase. To answer my previous question, what is success, the answer is YOU are success. You are successful simply by being yourself and finding enjoyment and happiness in your being. There is nothing to chase, there isn't a race to be won, and there aren't any awards to be handed out. The paradox here is that the more joy, love, happiness, and fulfillment that you find in each and every moment, the quicker you will achieve your goals. Goals are a great thing to have, but don't let them define you and define when you will finally arrive at a place of so called success. Success isn't an external circumstance that you will one day achieve. Success comes from the inside and originates from how you feel when you wake up every morning. Get out of the chase, don't get caught up in the hype, and in the long run you will reach your goals along the way.

Consider a Spiritual Approach Rather Than a Psychological Approach

Our culture is obsessed with psychoanalysis, whether it

is in the form of trying to figure out what your boyfriend is really thinking or feeling, watching an episode of Dr. Phil, taking a personality test, or simply reflecting on your own feelings and behavior. As human beings, it is our nature to search for the how and the why. We want to make sense of why other people do what they do and have an explanation for everything. Especially when it comes to self-reflection, we all want an explanation to why we are who we are, why we struggle in certain areas of our lives, and why we do what we do. We try to find reasons why we can't make a relationship last, why we pick all the wrong partners, why we feel inadequate, hopeless, insignificant, etc. We run the tapes of our past (typically our childhood) over and over in our head looking for answers to these questions of why. We go to therapists, psychologists, and psychiatrists hoping they can provide some insight into the why.

Psychoanalysis can be very helpful, but it can easily be over-utilized and turn detrimental. So much energy is focused on this quest for self-analysis, and in essence, during the process you are giving all of your personal power to your past, which is a time that doesn't even exist in the here and now. It is rather easy to become so distracted by the analysis of your past that each present moment slips away and you never take action to actually move yourself forward. The psychoanalysis strips you of your power and it confines you to the story of your past. If you want more of the same, then lose yourself in as much psychoanalysis as you want, but if you want different results, if you want to take your life to a different level, if you want your dreams to become a reality, then it is necessary to take more of a spiritual approach to self-improvement and self-help. Instead of analyzing and casting judgment on every thought or feeling that you have and trying to pinpoint an explanation for it based on your past, simply observe them. Notice them. Don't try to interpret every single thought and feeling, but rather step back and observe them. When you can simply observe something, it doesn't have control or power over you.

If you can change your approach from a psychoanalytical standpoint to an observation standpoint, your past will no longer determine your future and you will be free to take action, effectively use your personal power, and begin to make your way on the road of success. Take control of your future by observing your thoughts and feelings. Understand that feelings of doubt, anxiety, fear, worry, and insecurity are part of the human experience. These feelings may always be with you but they don't have to paralyze you in your tracks. Notice them, but keep moving forward towards your goals and dreams.

God is Love, Not Thought

Regardless of your religious affiliation and religious school of thought, for everyone who believes in God, I think it is fair to say that one thing we can agree on is this: God is love. The statement God is love is well saturated in pop culture, the Bible, and various other religious publications. Sometimes I wonder if because this statement is so prevalent and over-saturated in our culture, that we have lost a sense of the power and truth behind this simple phrase. With that in mind, I would like to talk about how you can better understand more of the meaning behind the phrase, God is love.

To start, let's talk about what love is. I remember as a kid one of my favorite books was a book called *Love is...* and it had Snoopy in it. On each page, the author gave an example of what love is, for example on one of the pages it read Love is....giving a friend a flower. And for whatever reason that book stuck with me. Perhaps it is because love is one of those things that can't be fully labeled and identified by thought. It is as if love transcends thought, therefore it can't be fully explained or categorized by thought. Love just is. We can feel love, we can recognize love, and we can all give examples of what we think love is, but when it comes to thought and definition, love can be defined in a number of ways, and all of our definitions point back to the intention of trying to encapsulate the feeling of love. The Merriam Webster dictionary tries to define love 9 different ways.

Sometimes when you are trying to define a concept it is helpful to understand what it isn't, so let's discuss what love is NOT. I would like to point out that the phrase, God is thought, is not documented anywhere in history. God is definitely NOT thought. God can be expressed through thought, but in essence God is not thought nor is God any derivative of thought. Judgments, opinions, perspectives, and various points of view are derivatives of thought. Remember, God in essence is not thought, therefore God is not judgment. The judgments that you make of other people, other situations, and events are simply a product of YOUR thoughts. When we entangle God in our judgments, it is easy to become very intolerant and discriminatory of other people and events, and we do it in the name of God. This narrow-mindedness can very much hinder you on your road of success, bliss, and peace. You begin to build a mental prison built solid of your judgments of other people and events.

God is love, not thought. Thought is what you bring to the table. Make an effort to not narrow the playing field by building these ignorant prisons of judgment that you believe to be endorsed by God. In business, you might be narrowing your potential buyers and business partners, in life, you might be narrowing potential friends and allies, and in family, you might be isolating your children, brothers, or sisters for reasons only within your own mind. If you believe in God, you believe in love. Exercise the law of love in your life and increase your self-awareness around the fact that God is not thought. God is love.

Part 3

Be a Visionary

As little children, our mind was very much dominated by our imagination. We knew very little about logic, analysis, or complexity. Life was simple. We hoped to get our needs met through our caretakers, and the rest of our attention was focused on magic, fantasy, creativity, and imagination. We knew no limits, but as time went on we began to quickly realize that our creativity and imagination didn't have a place in this thing called reality. Growing up, some of our parents' favorite words included can't, don't, or stop. We quickly became accustom to following the rules because that is how we felt safe and enjoyed rewards as well. Unfortunately, one of the main consequences of being socialized and learning to follow the rules is that your imagination wanes, and you begin to place more value on developing your ability to analyze, organize data, problem solve, and stay within the unspoken boundaries of society.

Successful individuals are able to maintain and develop their ability to imagine and dream. They understand the importance of having the best of both worlds, meaning they develop their intellect, but also allow their imagination and vision to be part of their experience as well. They realize that their imagination is the driving force behind their ability to create goals. With their imagination, they can see the finish line before they even get there. This allows them to stay focused on their desired outcome and have a sense of what it will feel like when they reach their desired destination.

Being a visionary is an important part of the spectating role in being successful. Before any action takes place, you must first envision and create the mental equivalent of what you want to manifest in the physical world. Remember, your physical world is simply a reflection of your inner world. Your task is to take more control of what is happening in your inner world so that you can create the desired results in your life. This chapter will give you a better understanding of what it means to visualize and how it can improve your results immediately.

Visualization

The power of visualization has been documented and talked about for decades, but very much underutilized. Albert Einstein once said," Imagination is everything. It is the preview to life's coming attractions." Visualization is the act of creating mental images in your mind, and it is an excellent tool in accelerating your success. Researchers have found that your brain uses the same identical processes when you visualize an activity as when you are actually doing it in real life.

One of the key advantages of using visualization is that it activates the power of your subconscious mind. When you visualize your goals as already complete, you create a conflict within your subconscious mind because your current reality doesn't match your visualization. Because of this conflict, your subconscious mind is activated to assist you in turning your visualization into your actual reality. Your subconscious mind begins to bring helpful ideas and thoughts into your awareness. It increases your level of motivation and focus.

Visualization is a common practice in sports. Athletes all around the globe use visualization as a tool to increase their confidence, increase the consistency of high performance, and take their game to the next level. Golfers use this tool before every single swing they take. They visualize and think about where they want to hit the ball and how they will orchestrate getting that ball in the hole in the fewest shots possible. The most successful golfers plan out each hole and visualize how each shot will get them closer to their desired outcome. Now it is time for you to incorporate this skill into your daily life. Visualization isn't meant to only be used by athletes. Every single one of us can benefit from this skill.

You may find visualization difficult at first, but remind yourself that you were born with this skill. It is a part of your spiritual being that you can't lose, in other words, it is a part of your spiritual DNA. All you need to do is find a quiet spot, close your eyes, and see yourself achieving one of your goals. Maybe you have a goal of going to Hawaii for vacation. See yourself on the beach, visualize the sand. What color is it? Can you hear the waves crashing on the beach? Who is with you? What are you wearing? Do you feel the sun's heat on your face? While you are visualizing, make it as real as possible and visualize as many details as you can. It is as if you are creating a movie in your mind. You are the director, the starring actor, and you get to select the storyline. I would like to encourage you to take the time to visualize 15-20 minutes a day. Within 30 days, you will notice that there is something different about you and how you feel. You will feel more motivated, driven, and able to accomplish that goal. New ideas will come to mind, you will take appropriate action, then eventually your dream will be a reality for you. If you go there in the mind, you will go there in the body.

It is important to keep in mind that circumstances don't make a person, but rather they reveal the person. Life can be hard, and the road to success is often not a walk in the park. Many people give up on themselves and just don't quite cross the finish line. What do you think the difference is between someone who accomplishes their goal versus someone you decides to quit? Here is a scenario. Let's say that there are two individuals both wanting to start their own business. They both have a college education, they both have financing to get them off

54

the ground, and they are both more than competent to take on this new venture. As time goes by, they build a sound business model, pick a location for their business, and hire staff. They are ready to take on the world.

Unfortunately, both individuals face many challenges and obstacles. They aren't serving enough customers, their marketing budget is limited, and money is running out. They are both working over 80 hours a week to keep their heads above water financially and keep the business afloat. After a few months, one of the individuals decides to quit. This person is worn out and discouraged. The other individual keeps going. This person tries different things and brings on more people. Eventually sales and revenue start rolling in. Five years later, this person sells the business and enjoys the life of a millionaire.

Going back to my initial question - what is the difference between these two people? On the surface, you could make the argument that the person who didn't quit was willing to work for it, but that still doesn't answer the question. Why were willing to work for it? The answer lies in the power of visualization. The person who quit allowed them self to be overwhelmed with their present reality and couldn't see past what they were experiencing and observing. The business was struggling, sales were falling, revenue wasn't coming in, and from their point of view nothing was improving. Naturally, they were frustrated, discouraged, and eventually became hopeless. They were emotionally stuck and overwhelmed by the moment, and as a result they lost sight of their dream and lost sight of the bigger picture.

Regardless of whether you are opening your own business, wanting to climb the corporate ladder, or dreaming of being an actor or musician, you have to be a visionary. You must always keep the finish line in mind and never lose sight of it. I guarantee you that there will be times when you think you just can't keep going, it feels hopeless, and you might as well just quit. Those will be the moments that define you as a person and define your level of success.

Making Decisions

One of the best kept secrets in regards to being successful revolves around making decisions. If you want to increase the level of success and happiness in your life, make decisions based on where you are going, not where you have been. It is important to keep in mind that your current level of success and happiness, or lack thereof, is nothing more than the residual outcome of your past thoughts, feelings, and actions.

Your body, your health, your home, your bank account, you car, your marriage or relationship, your job, your happiness, or lack thereof, is simply a reflection of who you are. The results in your life, in every area, are a biofeedback mechanism to what you have been doing with your thoughts, feelings, and actions. Your life is a mirror of who you are at this moment. Using the analogy of a mirror, remember mirrors don't judge. Mirrors don't determine whether something is good or bad, nor is the perspective skewed in any way. Mirrors simply reflect back the image of what's put forth. Your life is a mirror image of your thoughts, feelings, and actions. Go stand in front of a mirror and think about what you see. Think about all aspects of your life including your health, your home, your relationships, your job, your bank account, etc. Think about the things you want to change and improve. As you think about this, it is important to understand that what you are looking at in the mirror has nothing to do with your potential and what you are capable of becoming, unless you accept what you see and continue to make decisions based on where you have been. You will simply create more of the same.

If you want different results in all areas of your life, then make decisions based on where you are going, not where you have been. Keep your desired outcome in mind as you make decisions on a daily basis. For every decision you make, ask yourself," Is my decision aligned with my goals and desired outcomes?" Every decision you make is either carrying you forward towards the life of your dreams or it is keeping you away from it. Incorporate this simple idea into your life and begin to make decisions based on where you are going, not where you have been.

Visualize From The Outcome

As I previously mentioned, wishful thinking alone isn't going to get you that beach house you constantly envision or that beautiful sports car that you so badly want to own. In order to get what you want, you need to act on it and work towards your desired outcome. To accomplish your goals as quickly as possible, you need to incorporate what you already know about the Law of Attraction and think, feel, and act from the outcome not towards the outcome. At first glance, you might be thinking that acting from the outcome is the same as acting towards the outcome, but they are drastically different. When you act towards the outcome, you are operating on thoughts starting with "I want…". An example could be, "I want to have a beautiful house right on the beach." or "I want to lose 10 pounds.". When you are acting from the outcome, you are operating on thoughts that start with "I am…". For example, "I am enjoying my new house right on the beach." or "I am 135 lbs, and I love it!".

Let me explain how the Law of Attraction reacts to these different sets of thoughts. When we have thoughts of "I want", we are re-enforcing the lack in our life because when we say we want something, it sends out the message to the universe that we don't have it yet, so keep it that way. When we have thoughts of "I am", the Law of Attraction has no other choice but to bring into our lives because our vibration matches the essence of what we are trying to attract. As a result, when you are thinking, feeling, and acting from the outcome, the universe delivers. Here is an example to illustrate how this works. Let's say that you want to lose 15 lbs and become really fit. If you were acting from the outcome, here is what you would do: first, based on your knowledge of the Law of Attraction, you would create a simple affirmation that you would say to yourself every day. Your affirmation would start with "I am…". An example could be, "I am enjoying my lean fit body and my ability to feel comfortable in my clothes and look really good." Once you have decided on your daily affirmation, you would then start asking yourself some questions like: If I were a lean healthy person, what would I do on a daily basis? What foods would I choose to eat? How much would I eat? At what times of day should I be eating? How often would I exercise each week? You would start brainstorming while using your vision and imagination to shape what this new and improved version of yourself would look like and act like. Once you define that, you can then immediately start doing those things.

Lean healthy people usually exercise on a daily basis, eat foods high in protein, drink plenty of water, and get enough sleep. Because you have defined this new and improved version of yourself, you can now incorporate this new attitude and new habits into your routine. You become who you are trying to be by acting from the outcome.

Step Out of The Whirlwind

We live in a fast-paced world. Most of the time you probably feel like you are running just to stand still. The fact is your daily life and daily responsibilities are similar to a whirlwind. It is very easy to get caught up in the hustle and bustle of daily life. You live in a whirlwind in which all of your time and energy is devoted to keeping things going and managing the day-to-day. Unfortunately, as you live your life in this whirlwind, you are stifling the level of happiness, growth, and success that you will experience in your life. Life will simply pass you by. You will wake up 10 years later wondering where the time went and why you never went after your goals and dreams.

In order for you to progress and reach the level of success and happiness that you want, it is critical to find a way to make time each day to think about and act towards your goals and dreams while you manage the daily grind. Remember, we make time for the things we value, and every single one of us has the same amount of time during a day. Being short on time isn't one of those things that you can blame on socio-economic status or your parents. You are 100% responsible for how you manage the 24 hours that you are given every day. No matter whom you are or what kind of childhood you had, everyone gets the same amount of time allotted each day. Time is one of the few things in life, if not the only thing, where everyone is on a level playing field. You should feel comforted by that. Think about it, there isn't one other person that is better than you when it comes to time. Because of that, time management is a huge arena where you can really differentiate yourself from the rest of the crowd.

All of us understand that time is of the essence, but so few of us pay attention to where our time goes. Where does your time go? A great way to get a visual of where your time is going on a daily basis is to take a few minutes before you go to bed and draw a circle. The circle represents a 24 hour period. Taking account for every hour, figure out how many hours you are dedicating to the various activities and responsibilities throughout your day and demonstrate it similar to how a pie chart is used. How many hours are dedicated to work? How many hours are dedicated to sleeping? How many hours do you spend cleaning the house, playing with the kids, etc.? How many hours are spent each day working on your goals and dreams? Make sure to account for every hour within that 24 hour period. This quick exercise gives you a very clear picture of where your time is going each day, and it allows you to find areas that could be cut back in order to make room for time spent on your personal goals. Are you spending your time on things that are important to you? What keeps you in the daily whirlwind of life?

Your time spent is a clear indicator as to what is important to you. Things that aren't important fall to the wayside whether it is your relationships, job responsibilities, activities, cleaning, etc. If it is important to you to achieve your goals and live the life you have always dreamt about, prove it by making time for it. Take a look at what you wrote down and figure out where you can make some adjustments to your time schedule. How much sleep are you getting each night? Could you manage getting up one hour earlier to make more time available? How much time do you spend watching television? Is the television show more important than your personal goals? Take a look and figure out where you can cut corners and open up more time. You must get beyond the daily whirlwind, step outside of it, and invest in yourself and your dreams. Make the time to work toward your goals. Start small and take an hour a day. Over time, set deadlines for yourself.

This will create some momentum and personal accountability. Go for it. Step out of the whirlwind and onto the pathway to your goals and dreams.

<u>Be Creative, Not Destructive</u>

As beings of consciousness, our nature is to grow, expand, and create. In fact, it is the nature of the entire universe and everything in it. Because we have an innate desire to expand and grow, we are constantly moving, whether it be up, down, left, right, or perhaps around and around in circles. We expand, we contract, and we breathe in and breathe out. There is constant energy movement whether it is on the surface or underneath it all.

There is a universal law that states," If you're not growing, you're dying." I would like to apply this principle to the idea of creation and destruction, which has similar connotations. One could restate the universal law and say," If you're not being creative, you're being destructive." We all know who the "destructive" people are. They are the complainers, the energy vampires, the pessimists, and the downers. They can identify every problem that exists in their life, your life, and the world within a matter of minutes. They can give you 100 reasons why something can't be done. You spend one afternoon with one of these folks, and you are completely mentally exhausted and depressed. Individuals that operate from a destructive mindset tend to always see the negative and are quick to bring you down emotionally or tell you what you do wrong. Sometimes it might feel like their goal is to chew you up and spit you out while destroying any ideas or dreams that you have. On the other hand, individuals that operate from a creation mindset tend to always see the positive and are willing to help you along your path to success while supporting new ideas and concepts. They are the optimists that wear rose-colored glasses and find opportunity in challenging situations.

Because success is all about creation, it is important not to have a destructive mindset and to also rid yourself of individuals that carry this destructive mindset. If necessary, get them out of your life or at least limit your exposure to them. If you allow the destructive way of thinking to permeate your mindset, you will be left picking up the pieces and your ability to create will be useless. If you are not operating from a creative and positive mindset, chances are you are allowing yourself to be destructive. Pay attention to your words and your deeds. As you go about your day and communicate with others, are your conversations of a creative nature or a destructive nature? Are you focusing on the problem or are you working on a solution?

Build people up, build yourself up, and by default, you will be well on your way to building your success. Incorporate this universal law of growth and death by constantly asking yourself, "Am I growing or dying? Is this thought or feeling creating my success or is it destroying it?" Create your goals and dreams through creative thinking. As you are faced with challenges along the way, always focus on the solution. With every problem, there is a solution. It is universal law. The challenge is that the solution doesn't exist at the same level of thinking as the problem. You have to think beyond the problem in order to get to where you are trying to go. You will get there with creative thinking.

Find Your True Passion

Regardless of where you live, you learn at a very early age the importance of money and how the amount of money that people have affects many aspects of their life as well as their children's lives. You are quickly judged by the amount of money that you make and you attach your self-worth to how much money is in your bank account. At an early age, I correlated money to power. It was evident to me that the more money you had, the more powerful you were and the more influence you had. Because of how our society is built and how we are socialized in re-gards to money it is easy to get lost in the quest to be rich. We are socially programmed to believe that money buys happiness and there is no if, ands, or buts about it. Unfortunately, this internal drive for wanting to make a lot of money will blind you from your true heart's desires and your true passion in life. This issue is often evident in medical students who were initially driven by the guaran-tee of earning a fat paycheck only to drop out of medical school because they don't have the drive or interest in it any more.

It is so easy to lose sight of yourself in this world, especially when it comes to money. In order to avoid this money trap, I would like to encourage you to ask yourself some serious questions. Sometimes identifying your true passion in life is so hard to do because it is difficult to separate it from the idea of money and what money can bring to your life. In order to find your true passion and focus your attention in the right direction, I am encouraging you to take some time to ponder on each of these questions.

1. If you were paid $5,000,000 a year regard less of your specific profession, what would you be doing? Make a list of everything that comes to mind. Write it all down.

2. After you have exhausted your answers to the first question, answer this: If all of your basic needs were met including food, shelter, clothing, and transportation regardless of your specific profession, what would you choose to do for your 40 hour work week? Make a list of everything that comes to mind. Write it all down.

After you have exhausted your answers, compare both lists. Identify which items landed on both lists. The items that made it to both lists are where your true passion lies. At that point you can really study those items and think about where you should go from here knowing that these items are the key to fulfillment and happiness in your life. The ironic piece to all of this is that if you find your true passion and work hard while having fun, money will follow. It truly is a win-win.

New Year Resolutions and Goal Setting

At the beginning of every year, our society gets excited and optimistic. If there is ever a time to make a goal, it is January. It is that time of year when we all feel compelled to create, what we like to call, New Year resolutions. There is always so much hype at the beginning of the year. As a culture we act as if it is the only time to make a valiant attempt to better and improve ourselves. Sometimes it feels like there is an unspoken rule that you shouldn't make an attempt any other time than at the beginning of the year. The truth is that every day is an opportunity to change and improve yourself. The time to grow is now, and it is always now, regardless of whether it is the beginning of the year, March 2nd, or August 3rd.

Setting goals and making New Year resolutions are great ways to focus yourself and get yourself moving in the right direction. Unfortunately, the majority of New Year resolutions fail and goals are often hard to reach because we often build them from wishful thinking. Why is it that most people can't even remember what their New Year resolutions were when asked 3 months later? Why is it that so many New Year resolutions shrivel and die before they are given a real chance to grow and develop? Why do individuals quit on their goals? The reason is because many intentions are built on wishful thinking alone. Wishful thinking isn't enough to accomplish a goal. Wishful thinking is empty, it lacks focus, attention, and strength. Nine times out of ten wishful thinking isn't even what you really want. You are simply thinking on a whim or impulse. Wishful thinking reflects more of what you are missing in your life rather than what you actually want. For example, let's say one of your friends is telling you about their new boat. They bought it a few days ago, and they are so excited. You can feel the excitement oozing out of their body! Well, in reaction to what you are feeling from them, you might think to yourself, "Geez, I should get a new boat. I want to feel that sense of excitement for myself." That impulsivity is an example of wishful thinking. Another example of wishful thinking would be if you saw an advertisement for a weight loss program and you think to yourself, "I should really lose some weight.", but you continue to eat as much as you do and hardly ever exercise. Wishful thinking contains fleeting thoughts that lack focus, attention, and strength.

Successful New Year resolutions, and really all goals for that matter, occur when you do three things. First, you must state a clear intention or goal. What specifically do you want to accomplish? If you want to lose weight, specify how much? If you want to make more money, specify how much? If you want to find a new job, specify what industry? Make sure that your intention or goal is specific and measurable. Second, you must focus all of your attention on accomplishing that goal. Energy flows where attention goes. What is your attention on? Keep your goal at the forefront of your mind. If necessary, write it down and look at it every morning and night. Third, you must act from the outcome. Begin to act as if you were already at the finish line. For example, let's say that your intention is to lose 10 lbs within the next three months. As a result, every morning you look at your goal sheet so that it reminds you of where you want to be. In order to act from the outcome, you should ask yourself, "If I were 10 lbs lighter and in better shape, what would be my food choices? How many times a week would I need to work out to maintain that weight?" Throughout your day, you should be making choices that support the mental picture of you 10 lbs lighter.

In summary, in order to reach your goals and resolutions, state a clear intention that is specific and measurable. Second, keep your focus and attention on it on a daily basis. Third, act from the outcome. As you implement this process, you will consistently reach your goals, and you will be well on your way to the life of your dreams.

Part 4

Relationships

We live in a world in which everything in our life is a direct reflection of who we really are, so our relationships are a great tool for self-improvement and insight. When you are ready to learn more about yourself and identify your strengths and weaknesses, all you need to do is look around you. No mirror required. Instead of looking in the mirror, it is more helpful to use your relationships as the mirror. Your relationships, which include connections with your family, your spouse, your kids, your job, your money, your car, your body, your clothes, and anything else that you come in contact with in your life, expose your trigger points and your hot buttons. Anyone can find peace and contentment while they meditate in a quiet space, but try to maintain that level of inner peace when you walk out your door in the morning and start interacting with people and things. How did it make you feel when that lady cut you off when you were trying to merge on the freeway? How did you react when your boss pulled you into their office to give you some constructive criticism? These are the experiences that allow you to learn how to better manage your reactions, emotions, and feelings.

Relationships allow you to get immediate feedback related to hidden areas of your soul that need development. It is an amazing tool to have at your disposal, but it is easy to ignore the lessons that can be learned through this mirror. It is important to be aware of what feelings and emotions that other people, things, situations, and circumstances evoke from within you. How do you feel when you visit your parents for the weekend? Do you experience anxiety and dread or do you feel a sense of excitement? If you experience anxiety or dread, why do you think that is? Could there be some unresolved issues between you and your parents? If so, that stagnant energy is affecting your ability to obtain success, inner peace, and happiness. These are questions that need to be addressed. Paying attention to the relationships in your life can give you that insight.

There is a great deal of spectating involved in using your relationships as mirrors into your soul. It requires stillness, contemplation, detail-orientation, and connecting with your inner needs. It requires you to be open to receiving constant feedback from your relationships and to have a willingness to investigate within yourself what could be the driving forces creating the dynamics (good or bad) in your relationships. As you read this chapter, try to maintain a high level of openness towards the role you are playing in the outcomes tied to your relationships. The human tendency is to get defensive and place blame on others, but try to rise above that as you begin to contemplate and learn from the mirrors in your life.

Your Reactions

Our existence is a series of outcomes strung together that weave in and out to create the fabric of our lives. As you experience life, you create many outcomes that encapsulate your level of bliss, quality of life, and inner peace. Outcomes are defined as an event or experience and your reaction to that event or experience. Viewing an outcome as a mathematical equation, it would look like this: $E + R = O$. The "E" is the event, the "R" is your reaction, and the "O" is of course the outcome. I was lucky enough to realize at an early age that my reaction to circumstances either allowed me to grow as an individual or held me hostage, but it wasn't until I read Jack Canfield's book, *The Success Principles*, that this idea really hit home for me.

Let's analyze this mathematical equation, $E + R = O$, because it powerfully illustrates the active part you play in determining your outcomes. Again the "E" stands for the event. The "R" stands for your reaction or your response to the event, and of course the "O" is the outcome. Now from a mathematical perspective, there is only one thing that is going to change the outcome - your reaction. Life happens and a lot of times you don't have much control over events or circumstances in your life, but you have 100% control of your reaction. Your reaction is the variable to this equation. If you want to control, change, or improve your outcome, your reaction is the key.

When it comes to your reaction to events and circumstances, you have two choices. You can blame the quality of your life on your unfortunate circumstances and waste all of your energy throwing your hands in the air as you play the victim or you can take a non-victim stance and change your reaction. As an example, let's say that you recently opened your own restaurant about 6 months ago, and business is stagnant. For the past six months, you have been putting the bulk of your advertising funds into neighborhood mailings and so far you aren't getting the results you need. Let's use the $E + R = O$ formula to see how the outcome could be altered. The event/experience is you opening your new restaurant and making an attempt to build your customer base. Your reaction has been the use of the neighborhood mailings, and unfortunately a lack of customers is your outcome. What do you do?

As always, you have some difficult choices to make. You could look for someone of something to blame and hold yourself hostage by the circumstances, you could continue to use the mailing service and get the same outcome, or you could change your reaction and do something different. You could try a different form of advertising. Again, if you want to change the outcome, your only choice is to change your reaction. Make sense? If you don't change your reaction, you will continue to get what you have always got. This concept can be applied to all areas of your life, whether it is personal or business. Think about the outcomes that you are creating in your life and think about which ones you want to change. Make your best effort to take control and avoid a victim mindset.

Your Relationship with Money

Your relationship with money will ultimately determine the level of prosperity that you experience in this life. Money is always a very interesting subject to talk about with people. I have come to realize that money takes many different forms in peoples' minds. Some people love money, some hate it, and others feel uncomfortable, guilty, unworthy, angry, or hopeless when the subject of money is opened. Some individuals pretend to not care about money as a method to hide their fear and insecurity. Their apathy towards money eliminates the potential of failure that they might feel if they never make a lot of money in their lifetime based on their personal expectations.

The truth is, regardless of your current relationship with money, it is a part of reality for anyone living in a civilized society and your mindset around it is going to determine the flow, or lack thereof, in your life. One of the most effective ways to improve your relationship with money is by paying attention to your emotional responses around money and make efforts to change your existing beliefs and thoughts that are triggering the emotional responses. As I have previously mentioned in this book, your thoughts, beliefs, and mindset create your reality. The results in your life are a direct reflection of your past thoughts and habits. In regards to money and abundance, you either have a scarcity mindset or a prosperity mindset. For many of us, it is very easy to form and get stuck in a scarcity mindset where we constantly see lack and limitation in everything. We are programmed from an early age that money doesn't grow on trees, rich people are only those who deceived their way to the top, life is a struggle and was meant to be a struggle, and being poor is noble. I could go on and on. These are all lies. In addition to all of the lies that we are exposed to, we have people constantly telling us what they think we can't do or perhaps how difficult something will be. It is very easy to buy into all of the negative propaganda. Don't do it. If you do, you are sealing your fate of mediocrity and lack. Your life results will simply reflect your limiting thoughts and beliefs.

As Bob Proctor explains in his book, *You are Born Rich*, we exist in an ocean of thought-energy where all knowledge there ever was or ever will be is present. We are surrounded by abundance. The only lack that exists is conscious-awareness. If you want to diminish your scarcity perspective and create a prosperity mindset, you must open your mind and begin to think prosperous thoughts and create mental images of you enjoying the prosperity that is your birthright. Regardless of your current situation, if you ever want to be wealthy, you must change your thoughts and focus on the prosperity that you desire. Quit pushing the "playback" button and re-iterating your limiting beliefs and scarcity thoughts. You can choose to observe what is happening in your life, react to it and create thoughts in response to what you are observing or you can choose to formulate a new mindset focused on prosperity and abundance. Create a new reality for yourself by forming prosperous images in your mind, keeping your thoughts in alignment with the mental images that you create, and acting on those thoughts.

I would like to encourage you to take a good look at your relationship with money. Is it something that you constantly worry about? How do you feel when you open your bills? Do you focus on the lack of money in your life? Do you claim to not care? How do you feel about rich people? Do you feel jealous, angry, or resentful? What core beliefs to you have around money and how are they affecting the results in your life? Ask yourself these questions. If you want to experience financial wealth in your life, make the decision to change your mindset because mental awareness of prosperity always precedes financial wealth in the physical world.

Expand by Using the Mirror of Relationships

Our relationships greatly impact our lives and the level of success and happiness that we experience. Understanding how to create and maintain healthy and positive relationships is an extremely advantageous skill to have. When it comes down to it, we are all extensions of universal energy experiencing a unique and personal point of view. Underneath it all, we are all the same. In order to use your relationships as a platform for spiritual evolution, you must learn to see yourself in the reflection of other people. It is important to understand that the people who you have relationships with, regardless of whether these relationships are platonic, romantic, family-related, or work-related, they are a direct reflection of yourself. You act as a mirror for others and others act as a mirror for you. Through this metaphorical mirror, you can gain a great amount of insight related to your positive and negative qualities, and as a result create better results in your life.

As human beings, we are often attracted to people who exhibit traits similar to those that we embrace in ourselves, and on the other hand, we often dislike people who demonstrate traits that we deny or dislike in ourselves. For example, if an individual strives to be honest and embraces that trait, then they would dislike a person who is dishonest and have a strong negative emotional reaction to them. If an individual embraces the idea of being on time and punctual, then they would more than likely have a strong negative emotional reaction to someone who is consistently late because being late is a trait that they deny in themselves. Who are you attracted to and who do you dislike? What traits are demonstrated by these individuals? Is it intellect, beauty, cheerfulness, sadness, power, rebellion, insecurity, disrespect, or anxiousness?

Whatever traits they may be, it is important to understand that those traits are also thriving in you. Having this awareness can help you identify and decide whether these traits are traits that you want to continue to develop or if they are traits that you would like to transform and change. For example, if you find yourself attracted to people that are sad, controlling, and unhappy, then you need to realize that these traits exist and are thriving in you. Ask yourself, "Are these traits going to get me to where I am trying to go and allow me to achieve my dreams?" If the answer is no, then you have some work to do. And of course you could ask yourself the same questions in regards to people that you dislike and have a strong negative emotional reaction to.

This mirror of relationships is a tool that you can use to identify traits that exist in yourself so that you can decide which traits you want to develop or discard. We are multi-dimensional beings and every single one of us has positive and negative qualities. When we are willing to embrace both the positive and negative sides of ourselves, we can only then begin to further develop our own being as well as connect better with others realizing that they are simply a reflection of ourselves. Use your relationships to better understand the qualities and traits that exist within yourself, and I guarantee that you will be well on your way along the road of success.

Your Circle of Influence

In order to be successful, it is important to understand what you can control and what you can't so that you keep your attention in the right area. Sometimes it is easy to focus all of your attention on things that you don't have any influence or control over. It is a waste of energy. To help you better identify what they can influence and control, there is a simple exercise that I would like to share with you. For this exercise, I would like you to write down everything that comes to mind that is concerning to you. This could include things ranging from the economy, the stock market, your job, your friends, your family, neighbors, classmates, interest rates, and even those things that other people might tell you that are none of your business. Now that you have your list of items that concern you, I would like you to draw a big circle on a piece of paper and label it your "circle of concern." Now within your circle of concern, I want you to draw another circle and I want you to label it your "circle of influence". This circle, located within the circle of concern, encompasses all of the things in your life that you have influence over whether the influence is direct or indirect. Looking at your list that you created of items that concern you, for all of the things you have influence over, put them in your circle of influence. For all of the items in your list that you do not have influence over, put them in your circle of concern. Which circle has more items in it? Where do you focus the bulk of your attention? Is your attention being pulled by things in your circle of influence or your circle of concern?

The lesson behind this simple exercise is when you focus your attention and power on things within your circle of influence, you are maximizing the power within yourself to better and improve yourself and your life. If you allow yourself to get lost in your circle of concern, you not only weaken yourself but you also deny yourself the opportunity to find the answer within your circle of influence. As a result, you remain stagnant as your energy is focused on things outside yourself. It is important to pay attention to how much your attention gets pulled into gossip, hype, the headlines, or negative thinking. If your energy is directed on things outside yourself and your influence, you are simply wasting your energy and your time. Clearly define your path for success and happiness and keep your focus and attention within your circle of influence.

Energy Vampires

The entire universe is comprised of energy manifested as light. As a matter of fact, you are 99.99% light. Your body, mind, and soul are pure energy as well as everything else in this universe. Thoughts are entities of energy as well. As we live our life, we are constantly interacting with other bodies of energy whether they be people, objects, ideas, thoughts, foods, books, or movies, and as we interact, we affect each other either in a positive way or a negative way. Put simply, there are two categories that bodies of energy can fit into. One category includes anything that uplifts and empowers you, and the other category of energy includes anything that sucks your energy dry. I like to call this second group the energy vampires. These energy vampires suck every last bit of energy from you until you don't have any more to give. Items in the energy vampire category could include people, objects, thoughts, foods, books, movies, animals, etc.

The energy vampires in your life weaken you as they watch your goals and dreams pass you by. They suck your time and your energy while leaving you with a heavy heart and a sense of lack. An example of an energy vampire could be someone that you know that is constantly complaining, talking about lack, being critical and judgmental, moaning, and being pessimistic. Regardless of the situation, their perspective is half-empty. For every positive thought that you bring to the interaction, they have ten negative thoughts as a rebuttal. I am sure that you can think of someone in your life right now that perhaps fits that description. After you have a conversation with an energy vampire, you feel drained, perhaps even a little dazed and confused. They sucked you dry.

Another example of energy vampires are negative thoughts. Your thoughts either instantaneously give your mind, body, and spirit energy or take some of it away. When you worry about things in your life that you don't want, you are weakening yourself instantaneously and your dreams begin to fade away as the energy vampires, which in this case are your thoughts, suck the life right out of you. Energy either empowers or weakens you. When you focus your attention on the problems of the world, the struggling economy, crime, lack, or your debt, you are allowing energy vampires to steal away your dreams. If you want to taste success in your life and reach your potential in prosperity, abundance, and happiness, there are two things you must do. First, you must completely submerge yourself in things, ideas, knowledge, and books related to personal growth and what you want in life. If you want to have a successful business, lose yourself in it and focus all of your attention on your vision and goal. Secondly, you must avoid anything that weakens you. This includes avoiding people who are constantly complaining, bitching, and moaning about the lack in their life. Perhaps they are abusive, mean, or disrespectful. Let them go and stop allowing them to take your lifeblood. Avoid weakening thoughts of worry, lack, anxiety, and stress. Turn your attention back to your vision and goals. Think about the successes that you are already experiencing in your life. Focus on the prosperity and abundance that you already have. Be grateful. As you develop an attitude of gratitude, more good things will find you. If you do these two things, you will be well on your way on the road to your success.

<u>Stress</u>

Recent generations have slowly accepted stress as a way of life. It is as if you aren't normal if you aren't stressed out. It has become cool to be stressed and people often use stress as a badge of honor. Our society has promoted the need to feel stressed in order to sell products that guarantee stress relief. In actuality, we have a choice to feel stress or not. We create it ourselves based on our reaction to what is happening around us.

Stress has been defined as the body's response to a change that requires a physical, mental or emotional adjustment. It has been stated that stress can come from any situation that makes you feel frustrated, angry, nervous, or anxious and is caused by an existing stress-causing factor or stressor. This definition is helpful, but I would like to point out why these statements are somewhat misleading and I would like to give you a better understanding of what stress is and how it affects your life. In the above statements, there is an underlying notion that stress originates from an external source, meaning it is caused by a "stressor" that is outside yourself. This is incorrect. Stress originates from your reaction to the situation or thought and determines your ultimate outcome. All stress is determined and generated by your attitude and response to every situation. Your reaction activates the signs and symptoms of stress and the physiological response of your body. You either choose stress or you don't. You have the choice.

Regardless of the circumstances or situation, you have the choice to either activate the signs and symptoms of stress or laugh about it, accept it, and figure out where to go from there by getting creative. Stress not only is a dream-stealer it also affects your health and well-being. The more stress you allow in your life the weaker you become and you open the door to getting sick either on a short-term basis like having a cold or possibly even a long-term basis like a chronic illness. Stress weakens you and steals your attention away from your potential. Your mind is occupied with worry, anxiety, and pessimism. All of these emotions hold you stagnate in behavior patterns that won't get you anywhere. Start paying more attention to your reactions to "stressors" in your life. See it as an opportunity to breakthrough to a new level of understanding and behavior. Accepting stress in your life means you are resisting the present moment. You are attempting to resist what's in front of you. Accept it and take the bull by the horns. The more you accept the present moment, laugh about it, and react creatively towards it, not only will your stress levels go down but you will realize that your new mode of operation is allowing you to get more done, feel healthier, and experience more joy and happiness in your life. Let go of the stress and get in the fast lane towards your goals and dreams.

Power of Relationships

Regardless of whether a relationship is platonic or romantic, there are two simple, yet profound, concepts that have the power to shape each relationship that you have, and if you apply these two concepts to your life, you will create meaningful and lasting relationships. The first concept that you need to understand is that your relationships are either growing or dying. There is no such thing as stagnation or what some people like to call "coasting along". We do not live in a vacuum. Life is dynamic and the only thing that is constant is change. The direction of change that is occurring in your relationships will determine whether they are growing or dying.

Metaphorically speaking your relationships are like flowers. If you nurture them with love, sunlight, and water, your flower will bloom into a beautiful creation, but if you ignore it, don't nurture it, and don't give it water and sunlight, the flower will wither and die. There is no exception to that. If you do not tend to your relationships, they will wither and die. Your relationships take effort, love, and attention, so if you are unwilling to give those necessary ingredients, your relationship will be tumultu-ous, unsatisfying, and short. If you want your relation-ships to succeed and stand the test of time, make spending time together a priority. Ask yourself at the beginning of each day, "What can I do to nurture and grow the relation-ships in my life? What can I do to nurture the relationship with my kids or my wife?" And after you answer those questions, follow through and do it.

The second concept that you need to understand in order to have a lasting and fulfilling relationship is that the quality of your relationship is greatly determined by where you put your attention. Relationships have a rhythm that is solely determined by your attention and whether you are putting your attention on the other person's faults or on their strengths and positive characteristics. Based on quantum physics and the laws of the universe, you get more of what you put your attention on. Put simply, your attention magnifies and multiplies what you focus on. If your attention is on your partner's faults and shortcom-ings, you will generate emotions and feelings that will destroy the relationship. If you focus your attention on your partner's positive characteristics, you will generate positive emotions and feelings within yourself that will allow you to grow and nurture the relationship. You need to choose which side you are going to feed with your at-tention, the negative or the positive. It will be a constant battle within yourself that you will need to overcome in order to have a happy and long-lasting relationship.

There is a legendary story that very clearly illus-trates this point and talks about this battle between positivity and negativity that I would like to share with you. This story can be applied to relationships as well as any aspect in life. One day a Cherokee elder told his grandson about this battle that goes on inside everyone's head in regards to seeing the positive versus the negative, and he said,"My son, the battle is between the two wolves that live inside us all. One is unhappiness. It is fear, worry, anger, jealousy, sorrow, self-pity, resentment, and inferiority. The other is happiness. It is joy, love, hope, serenity, kindness, generosity, truth, and compassion." The grandson thought about it for a minute and then asked his grandfather, "Which wolf wins?" The Cherokee grandfather simply replied,"The one you feed."

If you want to have successful, happy, and fulfilling relationships always remember to nurture your relationships with time, love, and appreciation with the understanding that they are either growing or dying. Use your attention to feed the positive aspects of your relationships, and make sure you are feeding the wolf that you want to win. Choose happiness.

The Lesson and Miracle of Acceptance in Relationships

Your relationships, or lack thereof, offer an opportunity for self-reflection and growth. Relationships can either bring a significant amount of joy and fulfillment into your life or they can become your worst nightmare if you allow yourself to get stuck in unhealthy patterns. Acceptance plays a powerful role in your relationships, regardless of whether they are romantic, platonic, or professional. In general, acceptance can be defined as the act of receiving, reaching an agreement, or consenting to something. The absence or opposite of acceptance is resistance. Specific to relationships, acceptance can be further defined as the act of allowing or permitting. In other words, you are allowing the other person to simply be them self.

When you are demonstrating acceptance in your relationships, you aren't telling them what to do, you aren't trying to control them, you aren't trying to fix one of their bad habits, and more importantly, you aren't trying to change them. Again, you are simply allowing them to be them self. This is definitely easier said than done. An interesting point is a lot of people go into relationships thinking that they can tell the other person what to do or what to say. They try to control certain things, or they make it their mission to fix their character flaws, and quite commonly they think they can change the other person in some way. Often times, when individuals are in an unhealthy relationship or they are simply unhappy, the main idea that keeps them in the relationship is the hope that one day the other person will change, and they will be the one to change them. Gosh, all I have to say to that is good luck. Don't get me wrong, change is definitely possible, but what you need to understand is that you don't change the other person, they change themself, and quite honestly, I wouldn't get in the habit of waiting around for it.

By demonstrating acceptance in your relationships, it does a couple very important things. It provides a sense of safety, a sense of self, and a sense of unconditional love. Your spouse, partner, or friend is nourished in the relationship because they are comfortable knowing that they can be an individual as well as a part of the team, so to speak. The other key thing that acceptance allows you to do is it provides some mental and emotional space between you and the other person, meaning, it gives you the opportunity to truly step back, observe, and evaluate whether you want to be in the relationship or not. It allows you to self-reflect on how you feel about the other person, and it allows you to gain perspective on why the dynamic is the way it is. If you make a commitment to demonstrate acceptance in your various types of relationships, you will find that over a short period of time, your relationships will improve or you will lose interest and ultimately come to the conclusion that you don't need or want to participate in the relationship anymore. If your relationship was created on the premise of you trying to change or improve the other person, once you stop trying and accept them for who they are, there is a good chance that you will lose interest in the relationship and find the courage to let it go. You won't have a need for it anymore. The unhealthy dynamic will have been eliminated. So try it, give acceptance a chance and see how it transforms your relationships.

Part 5

Laws of the Universe

As a child, I learned very early on that every family was different, and for better or worse, I was stuck with the one I got. Being naturally inquisitive, I was constantly comparing, observing, and mentally making note of how my family was unique to other families. In essence, without realizing it, I was trying to find that intangible definition of normalcy and better understand how growing up in my family put me either at a disadvantage or an advantage when comparing myself to someone else.

Every single one of us at some point in our lives realized that money, privilege, and opportunity were not equal commodities out there for the taking. As children, our opportunity and success was very much dependent on the amount of money our parents made, how educated they were, their level of social skills, and their willingness and ability to support us in our endeavors. Your family plays a huge part in shaping your habits and personality and acts as a key component to the level of success you create for yourself. As a teenager, I had a hard time accepting that belief. I was resistant to the idea that my fate and level of success was going to be determined by my parents' level of success and ability. Even when evidence of this pre-determined destiny was thrown in my face time and time again, I still wasn't willing to believe it or accept it. It was clear to me that children of successful parents had a huge advantage on the road of success, but I wasn't willing to accept a position of disadvantage for myself.

Over the years, I became intrigued with success and what the difference was between someone who had money, success, and prosperity versus someone who did not. Clearly it wasn't just about the family you were raised in because plenty of successful, rich and happy people came from meek and poor beginnings. As I became more educated and experienced, I realized that not only do we need to take control of and better understand the inner world within our mind, but we also need to be aware of and incorporate the physical laws that govern our world and use them to our advantage. We live in a physical universe that is governed by laws in order to maintain the perfect balance between chaos and control. There are numerous universal laws that exist, but I am only going to highlight laws that by increasing your knowledge and understanding of, you can improve your life and increase the level of happiness, peace, and success that you experience.

As you play both the spectator and performer along your road of success, happiness, and peace, the more understanding you have of yourself and the world around you, the more you can anticipate and improve the quality of your existence. When it is time to perform and take action, this knowledge and awareness of the universal laws will ensure that you aren't working against them. All successful individuals use these laws to succeed whether they are aware of it or not. As you understand and apply the principles associated with these universal laws, you are choosing success and setting up the universe to work for you rather than against you.

<u>Law of Polarity</u>

According to the Law of Polarity, everything in the universe contains within itself an equivalent opposite. From a quantum physics perspective, every electron, which has a negative charge, must have a matching positron, carrying a positive charge. Everything contains poles or, in other words, opposites. In lay terms, this law states that there are two sides to everything and that opposites are simply different forms of the same thing. For example, hot and cold are varying degrees of temperature. Black and white are extremes associated with color. Black is simply a different degree of color as compared to white. As we relate this law to daily life, it is important to understand and accept that if something appears to be dire or heartbreaking, the equivalent opposite must exist within itself. The opportunity is ours to choose which pole we will focus and keep our attention on.

Napoleon Hill, the of *Think and Grow Rich*, made the statement, "Every adversity, every failure, and every heartache carries with it the seed of an equivalent or greater benefit." He was referring to the Law of Polarity. Again, this law states that everything in the universe contains within itself an equivalent opposite. It is scientific law. Let me give you a personal example to further illustrate this concept. When I was 20 years old, I was involved in an almost fatal freak-accident. It was a paragliding accident in which I collided with another individual mid-air and free-falled over 100 ft. My entire pelvis shattered causing internal bleeding and both my ankles suffered open-compound fractures. I was more than lucky to be alive and had a long road to recovery ahead of me. Similar to humpty-dumpty, the doctors had to literally piece me back together again and placed internal titanium hardware to keep things in place. From a negative perspective, this accident was heartbreaking. Not only did I have a long recovery ahead of me, but I wasn't ever going to have full-functioning ankles again, my mobility and strength would be limited, and I would never be able to run or jump. I had many reasons to be angry, frustrated, hopeless, and depressed. Now from a positive perspective, I was alive, I wasn't paralyzed, and I was under the care of some of the best orthopedic surgeons in my area. This was a perfect opportunity for me to pick which polarity I was going to focus my heart and soul on. I knew, that according to this scientific law, this tragic paragliding accident had within itself an equivalent opposite.

As heartbreaking and devastating this accident was, there had to be an equivalent positive, and that is what I chose to focus on. I used this experience to get me to where I am today and to embrace what it means to be truly appreciative and grateful of each and every moment in life. On many levels, I used my accident as a "start-over" button. On the physical level, I didn't have any other choice but to start over because I literally had to learn how to walk again – one foot in front of the other. On the emotional and mental level, my accident gave me the opportunity to really figure out what I wanted in life, what and who I needed to purge out of my life, and how I was going to accomplish my goals. I was more focused than I ever had been my entire life. I slowly cleansed myself of the chaos and conflict that attracted this accident into my life in the first place and off I went toward my dreams and goals. Today, I am very much at peace. As I was driving in my car the other day, tears of gratitude crept out of my eyes as I felt the peace of knowing that not only am I a survivor, but I was also able to reap many benefits and blessings from a devastating ordeal. I definitely got the last laugh.

As you apply the knowledge of the Law of Polarity to your life, make sure to look for the hidden blessings and opportunities that lie dormant in the trials and adversities that will come your way. Make the decision to find the equivalent opposite within the challenges in your life. They are there; it is scientific law. By keeping your focus and attention in the right direction, you will find that challenges and adversities will be easier to conquer and you will catapult yourself on the path of peace, success, and happiness.

The Law of Reverse Effect

Your subconscious mind plays a significant role in the creation of your reality as it works together with your conscious mind. Your subconscious mind acts on compulsion after taking direct orders from your conscious mind. As a result, the thoughts that you think consciously get etched on the pathways of your subconscious automatically. Because of this exchange, you can use your imagination and conscious thought to control and fully utilize the power of your subconscious and turn your dreams into a reality. While studying the interplay between the conscious and subconscious minds, a French psychologist by the name of Emile Coue discovered the phenomenon which is now known as the Law of Reverse Effect. Through much research and study, he realized that when your conscious desires and your subconscious mind are in conflict and not aligned with each other, your subconscious mind wins every time. In other words, if you hold a belief in your subconscious mind that is contrary to your conscious mind, the belief in your subconscious mind will drive and determine your behavior and success.

To illustrate this concept, suppose you were asked to walk across a narrow plank that was simply rested on the floor. You would do it easily knowing that there wasn't any real danger involved because the plank was very close to the ground. From a psychological perspective, your high level of comfort and confidence would be a direct reflection of your subconscious belief in your ability to walk across this plank. As a result, your conscious desire to walk across this plank would then be aligned with your subconscious belief that you CAN do it. Therefore you would make it to the other side of the plank successfully. Now let's suppose that this same plank was 50 feet off the ground and you were asked to walk across it. Depending on your fear of heights and belief in yourself, instead of feeling confident and comfortable, you would more than likely be engulfed with fear and self-doubt. Your imagination would start to run wild as it envisioned the possibility of falling or getting hurt. Your subconscious beliefs of self-doubt, fear, and physical limitation would come to the surface and impede your ability to focus and accomplish the task. This conflict between your conscious desire and your subconscious beliefs will result in an unsuccessful outcome because according to the Law of Reverse Effect, your subconscious beliefs and mindset will win every time and produce the outcome that is aligned with your subconscious mind. You might have a strong conscious desire to get across, but your fear of falling and failure would guarantee a poor outcome. The more you try to suppress and mask your subconscious beliefs, the more strength and attention is fed to them.

It is important to be aware of the Law of Reverse Effect so that you can recognize areas in your life where your subconscious beliefs are not aligned with your conscious desires. For example, if every time you are asked to speak in front of a group and your heart and mind are filled with fear and self-doubt, your body is telling you that your subconscious beliefs are not aligned with this task. You are lacking the confidence, skills, and beliefs that would guarantee a successful outcome.

As you recognize and become aware of these moments, the next step is to reprogram your subconscious mind. Remember, your subconscious mind is subservient to your conscious mind. Your subconscious mind takes your rational conscious thoughts and reacts and responds without bias. If you are thinking thoughts of fear and failure, your subconscious mind feeds it and gives you more justification to be afraid and works hard to create the image of failure that you gave it. In order to avoid this, you have to feed your subconscious thoughts and images that are aligned with your conscious desire. Specific to the narrow plank example that I mentioned above, as difficult as it might be, you would need to have that same confident feeling that you had when the board was a few inches from the ground as when it was 50 feet off the ground. You would want to visualize yourself walking across it successfully, looking straight ahead, completely confident. It would be necessary to satiate your subconscious mind with thoughts of confidence, success, safety, and ease and visualize yourself doing it.

In summary, if you want to get a desirable outcome, your conscious desire, imagination and subconscious mind must be in alignment. If a conflict exists between your conscious desire and how you feel, your results will be a direct reflection of your subconscious beliefs. Pay attention to this and as necessary, change your thoughts and use visualization.

The Observer Effect

Our entire universe is comprised of energy. Scientists have determined that on the quantum level, energy manifests itself in two forms. It either manifests as waves or it manifests as particles. Waves are the intangible form, whereas particles are the physical form. A scientist, Thomas Young, proved that energy manifested in the form of waves around the same time that Albert Einstein discovered that energy manifested itself as particles. In order to come to a resolution and make an attempt for common ground, the scientists at the time held a conference in Belgium to determine if energy manifested in waves or particles or both. There were two teams of scientists opposing each other. One team consisted of scientists from the Thomas Young way of thinking that were there to look through a microscope and prove that in the quantum domain energy manifested itself as waves. The other team consisted of scientists from the Albert Einstein way of thinking that were there to prove that energy manifested itself as particles. As a result, scientists on one side of the room were looking for waves and found waves, but no particles. Scientists on the other side of the room were looking for particles and found particles, but no waves. They were at a gridlock.

Not until someone from one side of the room convinced the other side of the room to look for the opposing element did they make any progress toward a resolution.

Many of the scientists who had only been seeing waves changed their intention and began looking for particles. Surprisingly, when they looked down the same microscope, instead of seeing waves, they now saw particles. The scientists were baffled because two minutes before when they were looking down the same microscope for waves, all they saw were waves. The scientists decided to look again with the intention of finding waves. Whoa, they found waves. They changed their intention again, back to particles, and particles are what they found. This concept is called the Observer effect. Simply put, the Observer Effect states that on the quantum level, which serves as a foundation of everything that exists in this universe, you get what you are looking for, no exception. An objective reality doesn't exist. The only reality that does exist is subjective, meaning it is tainted by our own intention, attention, and bias and all we ever find is exactly what we are looking for.

This is an extremely powerful discovery that affects you, your life, and your success. The Observer Effect proves that you will find and experience whatever your attention, intention, and focus is on. If you are looking for sadness, pain, challenges, things to be depressed about, you will absolutely find them. Now on the other hand, if you are looking for happiness, joy, prosperity, things to be excited about, you will absolutely find those as well. It is law. It is important to ask yourself whether you are focused on the successes in your life or if you are focused on your failures. Are you looking for solutions or are you completely focused on the problem. If it is a proven scientific fact that you get what you are looking for, why in the world would you want to ever put our attention on things that you don't want in your life? Use this law to your benefit and create the life that you want by choosing to observe and look for things that serve you and allow you to grow on your path to success.

Law of Vibration

The Law of Vibration states that everything in the universe is in a constant state of vibration. Everything in the physical world is energy vibrating at different frequencies. What differentiates a rock from a table is simply the frequency of their vibrations. Objects in physical form have lower frequencies as compared to thoughts. Thoughts are a form of energy that vibrate at the highest frequency. Because of their high frequency, thoughts can penetrate solids, time and space.

Many people use the word "vibe" without really putting much thought into it when describing a person or the atmosphere in a room. For example, someone might say, "She seemed like a really ornery person, and I didn't like her vibe." Without even realizing it, they are recognizing the fact that they felt her vibrations. Naturally, we all pick up on non-verbal communication and queue into the vibrations of an individual's energy. Successful poker players are very good at this. They pay particular attention to other players' energy, movements, and betting patterns.

The Law of Vibration gave birth to the Law of Attraction, which states that like attracts like and dissimilar frequencies repel. This is why our thoughts are so incredibly important. We get what we think about whether we want it or not. If we think positively and think about what we want, that is exactly what we get. On the same token, if we think negatively and think about what we don't want, that is exactly what we get. The Law of Attraction illustrates the power of our thoughts and attention, and it gives us a way to monitor our results based on where we are putting our attention. Energy goes where your attention is directed.

As simple as a concept this is, people are oblivious to the many ways that they are drawing attention to the things that they don't want in your life. Don't let this happen to you. In order to overcome this mental trap, I would like to introduce to you a very easy way to monitor your thoughts and behavior as it relates to keeping your attention on things that you want versus things that you don't want. Remember, energy flows where attention goes so to assist you in keeping your attention on the right things, I would like to introduce the analogy of a burning fire. When your attention is directed on something, whether it be something that you want in or life or something that you don't, you are mentally starting a fire. The more attention that you give it the bigger the fire gets. As you think about it, you are adding logs to the fire. As you talk about it with other people, you are adding logs to the fire. As you act towards it, you are adding logs to the fire. Each moment of attention that you give it, you are building your fire. Now this can work for you or this can work against you. If your attention is on things that you don't want in your life, you are mentally adding logs to the fire and allowing them to continue to burn and thrive in your life.

If there is something in your life that you don't want or is undesirable, take your attention off of it and place it on what you do want. Removing your attention is the only way to "put out the fire". Cut off the supply and quit putting logs on the fire through your thoughts, words, and deeds. Monitor yourself. Pay attention to your thoughts, words, and actions. Each thought, word, and action should be metaphorically adding a log to a fire that is positive in your life. If there are things in your life that are not in alignment with your goals and dreams, stop adding logs to those fires. Pull your time and attention away from them. You will see for yourself that as you withdraw your attention and focus from these unwanted things, the fires will simply go out. Put your attention on what you want in your life and who you are trying to become. You will be amazed at how much happier you will feel and how much faster you will be traveling on the road to your success.

Law of Gender

This law states that everything must have an incubation or gestation period. This gestational period is simply the time frame in which energy changes form. For example, the sperm and egg unite to slowly form a baby. The baby is the result of the transmutation of that energy. Another example of this law is the time it takes for a seed to break ground and grow into a beautiful plant or flower.

The key principle to understand is that energy is neither created nor destroyed. It simply changes form. Spring is one of my favorite seasons because it is an annual reminder of the Law of Gender. Flowers and plants are making their way out of the ground, while trees and bushes return to their full form. I am reminded of the powerful lessons that flowers, plants and trees teach us when it comes to what success really is and how to achieve it. The ancient philosopher Hermes taught, "As above, so below; as within so without". Flowers, plants, and trees give us great insight into this profound truth and allow us to visualize what this statement really means and how it relates to achieving results in our lives.

As you know, even the tallest of trees started out as a small seed in the ground. Before you even see evidence of the tree's existence, much work and preparation takes place during the gestational period as the tree begins to build a foundation for itself underground. As the tree grows stronger and bigger, so do the roots: as above, so below. The tree couldn't continue to grow if the roots didn't do its job underground. The Law of Gender directly relates to success in your life. If you want to experience positive results and success, it is imperative that you build and develop the necessary "root system" that corresponds and reflects the level of success you want to experience. There must be a gestational period where you are developing "the roots" that will eventually break ground and produce some amazing results. Success doesn't happen overnight and it doesn't happen without hard work. Metaphorically speaking, what's above directly corresponds with what's below. If you truly want to build long-lasting success and positive results in your life, the secret is to start building your root system. Similar to the life of a tree, as you develop your roots underground, in due time you will begin to see evidence of your hard work and dedication as your metaphorical success tree begins to show itself above ground in the form of positive results. Regardless of what your dream is or what your goals are, you must remind yourself of this universal law and ask yourself," How can I begin to build and develop my root system?" Remember, a huge part of your root system consists of your thoughts, habits, behaviors, and attitude, so if you are struggling on where to start, start there. Start with affirmations, start with meditation, and start with increasing your awareness and creating some space between your moods and emotions. Then when you are ready, do the work. Take the time to work on your goals even if it is just a few hours every day. Those few hours will eventually add up and your root system will create some aboveground results.

Because everything has a gestational period and you won't know how long it will take, it is imperative to have faith and believe in the unseen. Going back to planting a seed, you plant the seed with a complete expectation that it will grow. There isn't a doubt in your mind because that is what happens - seeds grow. It is important to use that same level of faith and expectation as you plant seeds of success in your heart and mind. Believe in yourself and have faith that you are moving in the direction of your dreams.

Law of Relativity

Einstein's Theory of Relativity states that everything in the physical realm exists because of its relationship to something else. I like to call this law, the Law of Comparison. Things exist without meaning until we compare it to something else and assign meaning. For example, cold only exists when compared to hot. If we didn't have hot as a point of reference, we wouldn't recognize cold. We can only define what cold is by using what we know about hot.

The reason this law is important to create success is that it is very easy to create and maintain self-defeating comparisons in your mind that affect the way you think, feel, and act. For example, let's say you make the conclusion that you are poor. In order to make that conclusion you use a point of reference to compare yourself and based on your point of reference, you can either feel poor or feel abundant. You are assigning meaning based on the point of reference you use. For example, if your point of reference is the income of a famous celebrity, you could feel poor even though you make over $100,000 a year. Now comparing your $100,000 a year to the average income for a small family in the United States, you are rolling in the dough. Depending on what you are using as a point of reference, your perspective completely changes, which in turn changes how you feel and act. What is so fascinat-

103

ing about this is because we assign our own meaning to everything, there could be two people living a similar life, but ultimately achieve a varied level of success and happiness. For example, we have two individuals employed in the same department and working in the same type of position. Individual "A" comes to the conclusion that her job is fun compared to other job opportunities available. Individual "B" comes to the conclusion that her job is awful compared to other job opportunities. Because Individual "A" is having fun at work, her performance level is very high. As a result, she receives a promotion that offers her higher pay and more flexible hours. Because Individual "B" thinks her job is awful, her performance is sub-par and she is overlooked for any opportunity. The difference between these two individuals comes down to their point of reference. The meaning that was assigned literally determined their fate and level of success.

The most powerful lesson to learn from the Law of Relativity is that you are the one creating the meaning behind an otherwise meaningless situation. Every day you are making comparisons and assigning meaning to every aspect of your life. These comparisons are shaping your reality and potentially holding you hostage. Remember, you are the one assigning meaning to an otherwise meaningless thought. If you are creating comparisons in your mind and feeling inadequate, insecure, or not good enough, you are holding yourself hostage because those feelings are setting in motion corresponding thoughts, feelings, and actions of lack, self-doubt, and insecurity. Use the Law of Relativity to your advantage and assign meaning that is uplifting and positive. When you notice yourself feeling compelled to compare and assign meaning, make comparisons that set in motion corresponding thoughts and feelings of prosperity, abundance, hope, and joy.

Law of Rhythm

The Law of Rhythm states that energy is like a pendulum constantly moving back and forth. According to this law, when there is a swing to the right, there must be a swing to the left. In other words, what goes up must come down. Everything has a cycle that it completes. For example, the sun rises and the sun sets, the moon rises and the moon sets. Each day turns into night and seasons come and go. Our bodies have their own rhythm when it comes to energy level, concentration, motivation, and thought patterns. Highs and lows exist everywhere whether it is in the stock market, your performance, your moods, or in nature. As you increase your awareness of this law, your decision making will improve as well as your ability to shorten the amount of time you spend in the downswing of the cycle. For example, every single one of us has bad days, feels down, or gets caught up in negative thinking. When you have more awareness around the Law of Rhythm, you understand that it is completely normal to feel down or to get caught up in negative thinking, but you have the choice to turn it around. You can quickly recognize your pattern of negative thinking and make a conscious effort to change. As you make those conscious efforts, you will spend more time in the upswing of the cycle and shorten the down-swing drastically.

Successful people know how to use the Law of Rhythm to their advantage. Professional athletes learn to recognize and adapt to this law so that they can maintain peak performance during important events in their career, whether it is the Olympics or the playoffs. Successful investors understand that there is a rhythm to the stock market and use that knowledge as part of their investing strategy. Learn to use this knowledge as part of your success strategy. Get to know your own rhythms, whether it be your mood, your energy level, or your thinking patterns, and make a conscious effort to impact the cycle.

Law of Perpetual Transmutation of Energy

The Law of Perpetual Transmutation of Energy states that energy is always moving and changing. Energy never stands still. In essence, change is all there is and there is no such thing as stagnancy. If you ever feel stagnant, it simply means you are going around in circles. Even things that appear solid and stable are moving and changing incessantly. This is evident when things are looked at under a microscope where we witness activity happening on the microscopic level.

Because of this constant motion, everything is either growing or dying. You are either moving towards something or moving away from it. This law applies to any concept, any object or any situation regardless of the circumstances. Everything in the physical world must comply with this law. To illustrate this, every relationship in your life is either growing or dying depending on where you are focusing your energy. There may be times when it is necessary to work long hours for a certain period of time, so as a result, your relationship with your spouse and family suffers. Eventually, work slows down and you begin to put more of your energy again into nurturing your relationship with your family and spend more quality time with them. On the flip side, there may be times when medical issues force you to take care of a loved one or family member and the relationship with your employer suffers.

The important underlying concept to understand with this law is that with every choice you make, you are putting yourself in motion. When you put yourself in motion, you are moving towards something and therefore pulling yourself away from something else. With every choice you make it is important to ask yourself, "Is this choice moving me in the direction of my goals and dreams?" If the answer is no, then clearly you are making the wrong choice. This is why having goals and having focus becomes so important. If you maintain your focus on your goals and what is important to you, you will always be moving in the right direction. If you don't have a focus or constantly second guess yourself, you will simply go around in circles and will easily be defeated by any challenges that come your way. Remember, energy is always moving, so make sure that you are putting your energy into the things you want. Because energy is always moving, change and evolution are always part of the equation. If you can learn to accept and embrace the fact that change is constant and that change is all there is, you will quickly adapt to it and eliminate the fear that holds you hostage.

Law of Cause and Effect

The Law of Cause and Effect states that every effect must have a cause and every cause must have an effect. In other words, this law describes the relationship between two events where the first event (the cause) generates the second event (the effect) and the second event is a consequence of the first. I remember learning about cause and effect in elementary school. It was a fairly straight-forward concept to learn. If "x" happens, then "y" will follow. Could it be any easier? Probably not, but the real question is why do you not use this simple law to make better choices?

Ultimately, your thoughts are the primary cause in your life. Your thoughts manifest themselves in your reality and create the effects in your life. Each effect that has manifested in your life can be traced back to the initial thought that started the chain of events. As you go about your daily life and make decisions, it is important to be aware that what you are creating and forming in your mind will manifest physically in your life. If you are thinking thoughts based in fear, anxiety, worry, or self-doubt, those thoughts will manifest themselves in your reality. If you are thinking thoughts based in confidence, love, peace, or abundance, that is exactly what you will get. Again, your thoughts are the ultimate cause in your life. Your reality has nothing to do with your parents, the economy, the opportunities that you didn't get, or any other excuse that might come to mind. The results in your life are a direct reflection of your thoughts.

As human beings, we tend to either ignore simple concepts all together or make things much more complicated than necessary, but it is important that you use the simplicity behind this law to make better choices in your life. Looking at the concept of cause and effect, we know that with every cause, there must be an effect and typically that effect could then be a cause of another effect. It is a continuous chain of events. You could very easily use this law to think through choices that you are making and decide whether the effect is really something you want. For example, let's pretend that you are making efforts to lose weight and make healthier food choices, but in one of your morning meetings one of your coworkers brings in fresh doughnuts. Oh no! Not only are they fresh, but they are from your favorite baker and have that infamous pink icing on top. As the box of doughnuts is passed around, your mind is racing. How are you going to handle this dilemma? Let's use the Law of Cause and Effect to help you through the decision process. If choosing to eat a doughnut is the cause, what would be the effect? Well, eating the doughnut would increase your carbohydrate intake for the day and add 300 calories to your daily caloric intake. You would then either have to eat less for the remainder of the day to make up for these calories or you would have to do some cardio exercise. If you choose to eat the doughnut, not alter your caloric intake and not exercise, then that will negatively impact your goal of losing weight. This is where you could ask yourself, "Is that (the effect) what you really want?" This is the pivotal question that you can ask yourself. By asking yourself what you really want, this allows you to determine the value of your dreams and goals and determine what is more important.

I encourage you to use the Law of Cause and Effect in your decision making processes. Understand that your thoughts are the ultimate cause in your life, and do your best to consciously guide your thoughts in the direction of your dreams and goals. It is scientific law that the effects in your life will be a direct reflection of the quality of your thoughts, so use that to your advantage. As you are faced with decisions throughout the day, remind yourself what you really want and what is important to you. Make the choice that is in alignment with your goals and dreams.

Part 6
Take Action

As important as it is to do the necessary mental work in order to bring your dreams into reality, you need to be aware that thinking along isn't going to get you anywhere and that ultimately as the positive affirmations, vision boards, and mental imagery are exhausted, it is necessary to actually DO something in order to bring your dreams into reality. Your positive thoughts and mental imagery set the stage and prepare you to take action, so now is the time to put your spectating aside for the moment and perform. Your observation, contemplation, stillness, and deliberate thought direction paves the way for right and effective action. Because you have taken the time to be a spectator and increase your overall awareness of yourself and the world around you, it puts you in a better position to get positive results when you take action.

It is important to understand that even though you are focused on taking action and performing, you must still be aware and ready to use your spectating skills. As you take action, there will be times when you don't get your desired result on the first try, so it will be necessary to learn from and improve upon the action that you take. Don't turn your mind off as you start to move your body. Be mindful and flexible as you contemplate what the best course of action is. Actions are the main vehicles that bring your thoughts, ideas, and dreams into the physical realm. Upon reading this chapter, you will have a better understanding of what taking rightful action is all about, how to avoid the pitfalls and traps of ineffective action, and the importance of aligning your actions with your desired results.

Your Built-in Success Mechanism

Every living thing on this planet has a built-in goal-striving device to help it achieve its goal, which in a general sense, would be to live. For the simpler forms of life, the goal to live simply means survival for both the individual and the species. In animals, this goal-striving device is limited to finding food and shelter, avoiding or overcoming hazards, and procreating to insure the survival of the species. For us, the goal to live means much more than that. As human beings we have emotional and spiritual needs as well, so as a result, our built in goal-striving device is much broader in scope.

In the book, *Psycho-Cybernetics*, Maxwell Maltz

explains how this goal-striving mechanism works within us and how we can use it to our advantage and reach our full potential. Every living thing has a goal-striving device, or in other words a success mechanism. This success mechanism that Maxwell Maltz explains in his book is very evident in animals. For example, a squirrel doesn't have to be taught to gather nuts, it simply does it. Nor does a bird need to take lessons in nest-building or navigation. Birds know when cold weather is coming and the exact location of a warmer climate. For animals, their goals are pre-established and related to survival and preservation.

As human beings, we have the power to form our own goals beyond basic survival and preservation. We are blessed with an imagination. We are much more than a creature, we are also a creator. With our imagination, we create a variety of different goals, and we alone can direct our success mechanism through the use of our imagination. Our success mechanism allows us to find answers to problems, invent, write poetry, attain more peace of mind, become a better version of ourselves, or achieve success in any activity that we choose. It allows us to "steer" our way to the goal or target by using information and data that it has previously gathered through past successes and failures. Each success is remembered for future use as well as each failure. For example, when a baby is first learning how to use its muscles, the difficulty in reaching for an object is very obvious. The baby has little, if any, stored information to draw on, so its hand zigzags, flops around a bit, until over time it reaches the object. During this process, its goal-striving device/success mechanism was gathering information and learning from the failures in order to eventually succeed.

Another example to illustrate this success driven phenomenon could be someone learning how to catch fly balls. At first when the ball is in the air, the individual doesn't have much information to go off of yet in terms of how the trajectory and the speed of the ball is going to affect the distance and location, but over time, as more and more attempts are made and the success mechanism gathers more and more information through the successes and failures, they eventually become really good at catching fly balls and instinctively know where the ball is going to be.

There are countless examples to illustrate how the success mechanism works, but I am confident that at this point you understand its mode of operation. As you gain more awareness of your success mechanism working behind the scenes, make sure to fully utilize its ability to catapult you on the road to your dreams. Because your success mechanism is guided by your imagination, it is important to not be afraid to dream and set goals for yourself. Visualize the goals that you want to achieve in your life, and understand that reaching a goal is a process. It is a journey in which you zigzag your way to your target as your success mechanism gathers information along the way through your successes and your failures. Failure is part of the process. You are guaranteed to fail along the way, so don't let it discourage you or derail you from your path. You have to fail in order for your success mechanism to gather enough information so that you can eventually succeed. Know that with each failure you are inching closer and closer to your goal and desired outcome as you incorporate the lessons learned.

Your Physical Body

As I have mentioned previously, you are nothing more than a product of your thoughts, and when it comes to your physical body, a lot of your habits and thoughts are completely visible to the outside world. As soon as you step out of your house, there is no place for your physical body to hide. Your physical body is a very visible and exposing aspect of yourself as compared to your emotional or mental schemas that hide beneath the surface. Your physical body exposes opportunities for improvement that exist in your psyche, namely your habits and your thought patterns, and it also is a conduit of energy. Your physical body is where your soul/energy lives and is what allows you to express yourself in many ways. In order to reach your full potential and experience inner peace, success, and bliss in your life, it is important to provide your soul with a healthy and vibrant body to work and live.

Going back to a basic concept, your results are simply a byproduct of your efforts and attention. When contemplating the health of your physical body, a question for you to consider is: Are you putting enough effort and attention to this area of your well-being and if not, why? If the answer is no, there are a number of potential reasons why you aren't taking care of yourself physically. One potential reason could include the fact that you don't value yourself and that you don't think very highly of yourself. In other words, you might have a low self-esteem. Unfortunately, a low self-esteem will manifest in your physical body as well as every other area in your life. Another potential reason why you aren't taking care of yourself physically could be due to the fact that you have a busy schedule and other things in your life take priority over being healthy. Perhaps you choose not to take the time to go to the gym and make poor food choices because of convenience.

When it comes to value, hypothetically if you were to sell your organs and body parts on the black market, your body would be worth over $45 million dollars. Now imagine buying an animal, a dog, or a horse for $45 million dollars. Would you feed it fast food every day? No, you wouldn't. You probably wouldn't feed it fast food once a week or even once a month. You would feed it the healthiest food that you could get your hands on. Your effort and attention would be completely focused on nurturing and protecting this $45 million dollar investment. You would take the time that was necessary, you would feed it the right food, and you would completely take care of it. On the contrary, if you questioned the value of your investment, you wouldn't put that much thought and effort into taking care of it.

Unfortunately, a lot of us question our own value. We don't realize we are walking around in a $45 million dollar asset. If you question your personal work and don't value yourself, you won't put any time and attention into

116

taking care of your physical body, let alone your spiritual body. One of my favorite businessmen, Donny Deutsch, has said in the past, "Good fitness means good business." The beauty about getting into shape and taking care of your body is that the habits and thoughts formed in the process trickle over to other parts of your life and increase your success. In order to get in the habit of working out on a regular basis, you need to develop time management, time organization, discipline, and persistence. All of those characteristics and habits are necessary if you want to be successful in business, so you are killing two birds with one stone and you are well on your way to improving your life. If you want to be successful and you are ready to take action, but don't know where to start, start with taking care of your body and getting in shape.

Align Your Thoughts With Your Actions

Probably at this point in your life you have realized that your dreams can't come true by thinking alone. In the book, *The Secret*, much attention is placed on our thoughts and how our thoughts relate to the Law of Attraction, but it is important to remember that taking action is another vital part of the success equation. Visualization and wishful thinking alone aren't going to get you that beach house that you constantly envision if you just sit on the couch all day and wait for it to magically appear in our life. The visualization will get you started thinking in the right direction and get you believing in yourself, but you also need to work towards the outcome that you want by taking action.

If you truly want to manifest your desires and dreams, it is critical that you align your thoughts and actions with your desired outcome. Your thoughts and actions need to be in harmony moving towards your selected goal.

Ultimately we are a product of our thoughts because our thoughts drive our actions. If you take a brief moment in self-reflection, you will see overwhelming evidence of this in all areas of your life. What you think about pushes your actions in a specific direction and determines your results. Your thoughts start a domino effect that triggers your feelings, actions, and habits, which in turn determines your results.

For example, let's say that you have a goal of getting a Master's degree in business administration. You are excited about it and begin visualizing and thinking about having that degree. You even create an affirmation related to this goal that you read every morning before you go to work. At this point, you are doing all the right things. You are visualizing, you are using an affirmation, but what if you don't take any action? Is the degree going to magically show up in your mailbox? You need to start taking action to complement your efforts. You could begin looking at admission requirements, picking a school, start studying for the admission test, look at financial options, etc. If all you did was think about it, nothing is going to happen. Remember, it is important that your thoughts are aligned with your actions.

Here is another example. Let's say that you have a goal to become debt-free within the next year. According to the Law of Attraction, it is important to keep your thoughts and attention off of your debt because that is what you don't want. In abiding by that law, you try to take your attention off of your debt and begin to form positive thoughts related to money, but every time you get the mail and open your credit card bills you stress out and feel anxiety about your debt. Your thoughts of lack, poverty, money mismanagement, and insecurity trigger your anxiety and stress. These feelings paralyze you and limit your ability to take action and investigate potential options to relieve your debt. Your thoughts and feelings are not aligned with your desired outcome, so you didn't even give yourself the chance to take action. When you align your thoughts, you are setting yourself up to take the appropriate actions aligned with your goal. If you pay attention to your thoughts, feelings, and actions while keeping your goal or desired outcome in mind, your dreams will become a reality and the universe will be at your command.

Face What Isn't Working

It has been said, "Facts do not cease to exist because they are ignored." In your effort to be successful, it is absolutely necessary that you get out of denial and face what isn't working in your life. As human beings, we often deny or ignore key aspects of our lives because we aren't ready or willing to deal with them. Unfortunately, this mindset of denial firmly holds us in a state of stagnation. Successful people face their circumstances head on, listen to the warning bells, and take appropriate action no matter how challenging or uncomfortable the situation might be.

In order to face what's not working in your life, you are going to need to do something that feels a little uncomfortable at first or is perhaps out of your comfort zone. For example, confronting somebody with the risk of not being liked, not settling for an abusive relationship, or perhaps quitting your job in the effort of going after what you really want. When you are realistic with yourself and face what isn't working, it takes courage and responsibility. When you take 100% responsibility for your life, you are more willing to make changes and facilitate growth. When you don't take full responsibility for your life, your attitude holds you stagnant and keeps you from the success you want so badly to achieve.

One thing I have noticed over the years is that when people get stuck in a state of denial or lack of responsibility, they are very quick to find reasons outside of themselves to explain why things aren't working. They are so transfixed on having explanations and finding people or circumstances to blame, they don't even think about solutions. They over identify with their current situation, remain a victim, and don't even allow themselves to get beyond it. As long as they can explain whose fault it is, that is good enough for them and they never take action to make things better.

Successful people are committed to being honest with themselves. They find out why things are going wrong and make attempts to fix them versus trying to defend their current position and explain why initially they did what they did. Successful people realize that failure is simply a stepping stone to success and they use it as a learning experience. It isn't about ego, nor is it about being perfect. It is about taking action, analyzing the results and taking full responsibility for them, then figuring out what the next best course of action should be. In life, only occasionally do you succeed on your first attempt. Life is a matter of facing the right direction then making multiple and perhaps slight course corrections along the way until eventually you get to your desired result. As part of this process, you must face what isn't working. Keep in mind, doing more of what doesn't work, doesn't make it work any better. You will continue to get the same results. Take the time to analyze and identify what isn't working in your life and create a course of action that is aligned with your desired outcome.

Persistence and Experimentation

Albert Einstein defined insanity as doing the same thing over and over again and expecting different results. Unfortunately based on this definition, we are all a bit crazier that we think. As human beings, we are creatures of habit and self-mastery, so we have the tendency to do the same thing over and over again. Have you ever wondered why in your personal life history often repeats itself? The answer is simple. Typically you think the same thoughts, and therefore create the same habits, which in turn produce the same results. This repetitive cycle occurs on the surface as well as deep within the constructs of your mind. For example, because of this compulsion of self-mastery, you could get sucked into a video game and play it for hours because you are fixated on the fact that you can master the game and defeat the villain. Your tendency for self-mastery takes over and all you can focus on in that moment is mastering the game. The trap that video games provide is that you can try, and try, and try again. You have an endless opportunity to master it. It all depends on how much time you have available. It is important to be aware of this human tendency so that you dedicate your time to worthwhile tasks and goals.

On a deeper psychological level, another example of this could be evidenced in your selection of a potential life partner. Perhaps, you grew up with a father that consistently criticized and belittled you, therefore as a child you felt like there was nothing you could do to please him. Unfortunately, in your effort to master this experience growing up with your father, as you begin looking for a life partner, you are going to be drawn to cold and critical individuals. In your mind, whether you realize it consciously or not, you are making an attempt to recreate the past so that you can mentally and emotionally become victorious and change the outcome. The outcome you experienced as a child resulted in you not being able to please your father. You tried and tried and tried, but nothing was ever good enough. Now that you are an adult, you are bound and determined to prove your father wrong. You can please male figures in your life. Unfortunately, because you are being drawn to people with similar mindsets as your father, you are doomed to fail. No matter how hard you try you won't be able to please the individual because of their hyper-critical nature, and your insecurities around not being good enough are validated once again. Your childhood experience was recreated, and unfortunately, so was the same outcome. History repeated itself. History will repeat itself over and over again until you realize this pattern that you are living is a result of a wounded heart and you look within yourself to heal it.

As human beings, we are programmed to self-mastery and forming habits. It is important to be aware and mindful of what results your habits are creating and to make adjustments as necessary. Persistence is critical to achieving success, but the important thing to understand is that persistence alone will not get you anywhere. Doing more of the same will NOT bring you different results. Don't get stuck in the cycle of compulsion and self-mastery. If what you are doing isn't working, you must change your actions in order to get different results. For example, let's say that you started your own business, so now you have the task of attracting customers. After some brainstorming, you come up with the idea of mailing out coupons. Well, so after a few months, you notice that your sales remain stagnant, but instead of doing something different, you continue to mail out coupons to people in your area. Month after month you mail out coupons with lackluster results. Six months go by, twelve months go by, but your sales are not increasing. One year later, you have to consider closing your business due to lack of revenue, but at least you were persistent, right? Your persistence pushed you right into the ground.

The lesson to learn here is along with persistence, it

is necessary to adjust and experiment with different ideas and thoughts. Persistence won't get you anywhere if you repeat the same action over and over again and you aren't getting the results you want. Be aware that because of your human tendency for self-mastery, you will be compelled to do the same thing over and over again expecting different results. To combat this tendency, you must step back and experiment. Try a different approach. If that approach doesn't work, try something else. Remember, your thoughts, habits, and actions have created the results you have right now if your life. If you want to change or improve your results in any way, you have to think outside your box and try new approaches.

Taking Responsibility

When I was a child, one of my older brothers taught me an early lesson about taking responsibility. At the time, I was unaware of the true wisdom hidden within this sentence, but now as an adult, I definitely get the message. Whenever I tried to give him an excuse and not take responsibility for something, he would say, "Excuses are like buttholes. Everybody has one, and they all stink!" Little did I know how hard it truly was to take responsibility.

It is intriguing to me to observe others try to dodge taking responsibility for their results and their life. Kids do it all the time. You walk into the kitchen and there is spilled milk on the kitchen floor. Once you start asking about it, each child points the finger at someone else. It's spilled milk; it isn't really that big of a deal, but no one

124

wants to own up to it. We assume that kids will grow out of the "blame game" stage, but unfortunately the blaming mentality often sticks into adulthood. We get so good at finding things to blame for our poor performance or poor results. When we are young, we start off with the dog ate my homework approach, but by the time we hit adulthood, we have quite a few excuse tricks up our sleeve. It is often someone else's fault as to why we can't make it into work on time. We can think of a thousand reasons why our parents are to blame for every dysfunctional part of our psyche. The excuse list goes on and on, but if you want to take your life and your results to the next level, you need to give up the blame game and begin to take 100% responsibility for your life and for your results. Please notice that I stated 100%. I didn't say 90%. You must take full responsibility. The questions you need to ask yourself are these:

• Do I take 100% responsibility for my life and my results?

• Can I think of any reason, besides my own doing, why I am not as successful and happy as I want to be?

When answering these questions, you might have said yes to taking responsibility for your life, but if you could think of a reason, outside of yourself, why you are not as successful and happy as you want to be at this point in your life, then you have been sucked into the blame game. If you can think of a reason that is outside of your own doing then by default you are not taking 100% responsibility for your life. Perhaps you can think of past events or circumstances to justify and explain why you aren't happy and successful. When you don't take 100% responsibility for your results you are placing accountability of YOUR life on someone or something else. There is only one person responsible for the quality of your life, and that person is you.

If you don't take 100% responsibility for your life, you automatically place yourself in a victim stance. Victim stances are incredibly ineffective because you are allowing yourself to be held hostage by someone or something else, and you are sending the message to the universe that you surrender your entire existence to circumstance. You are at the mercy of everyone else. It is as if you are locked in a room, but yet you are the one holding the keys. Because you lack the empowerment and are emotionally frozen in pain, fear, sadness, or hurt, you don't ever open the door. You remain a victim your entire life.

Well, you and I both know that we can't control other people, and a lot of the pain that we experience in our life is created through our interactions with others whether it is family members, parents, spouses, partners, friends, or even co-workers. It is very easy to blame our poor results on any of these folks. If you find yourself having the tendency to blame other people, one thing you must understand is people do the best they can with the knowledge, emotional maturity, and skills that they have at that moment. This is an important concept because it allows you to step back for a second while avoiding the victim trap and allow space for forgiveness. Your parents did the best they could with the knowledge, emotional maturity, and skills that they had while raising you. Perhaps, in all reality, they sucked or maybe they were awesome parents. Regardless, they did the best they could with the skills they had. Understand that and let any lingering resentment, bitterness, or pain go. You are only hurting yourself by not taking 100% responsibility for your life. People aren't perfect. I know I'm not. Again, we do the best we can with what we have at that moment.

Not taking full responsibility for your life keeps you from making any changes and you remain stagnant. If you believe that you are where you are in life because of some external circumstance, whether it be your childhood, your parents, socioeconomic status, or whatever, you are not going to make any effort to change and improve your situation. Your blaming beliefs and lack of responsibility become your life sentence. You can avoid this mindset by taking full responsibility for your life and using your accountability to motivate you to grow.

Obsession with Perfection

There is this misnomer out there that portrays the idea that perfectionists are more successful than non-perfectionists. The truth is that your obsession with perfectionism could be the very thing holding back on your road of success. There is a very fine line between perfectionism that is healthy and perfectionism that is destructive as it keeps you fixated on insignificant details.

Human beings have the tendency to develop an

obsession with perfection as a way to overcompensate for feelings of inferiority, low self-esteem, or low self-worth. If an individual is feeling inferior or believes they are never good enough, they might develop an unhealthy relationship with perfectionism in an effort to counteract their feelings of inadequacy. Typically when children grow up in homes where their parents are hyper-critical, demonstrate only conditional love and affection, or place high expectations on their behavior and performance, the children develop emotional patterns of anxiety, low self-esteem, low self-worth, and a habit of negative self-talk. These children feel like they have to be perfect in order to feel worthy, loved, and appreciated. This obsession with perfection can be very devastating personally as well as professionally. If this scenario hits home for you, than I would suggest you really take a look at your need for perfection and work on raising your self-worth and self-esteem. Until you do the inner work to eliminate your belief that you are not good enough, your life results will reflect that sense of lack and you will never achieve what you really want. You will always end up short.

An obsession with perfection can also be a reflection of one's driven, anal, type-A personality or a reflection of one's analytic, detail-oriented demeanor. For the anal, driven detail-oriented individuals, it is important that you don't get fixated on the details. The world moves way too quickly. If everything you do needs to be perfect, the world and your success will simply pass you by. You simply don't have time for perfection. Today's world is all about multi-tasking and being productive. Your expectation is to create good results while managing a lot of responsibility. Achieving good results on a consistent basis will catapult you much further than achieving great results every once in a while.

I tend to be a perfectionist, so it is important for me to be aware of myself and work hard to maintain a balance between creating good results and fine-tuning the details. One thing that I catch myself doing is if there is a project that I want to take on and it is something I haven't done before or don't have much experience with, I tend to put it off because my fear of it not being perfect paralyzes me. Eventually, I do get started and I muddle my way through it, but my need for perfectionism can stall my production. On your journey of success and happiness, pay attention to your need or obsession with perfection. It could in fact be hindering you and your progress in life. Remember, achieving good results consistently is much more power-ful than achieving great results every once in a while. The individuals that get the promoted are the ones that consis-tently get results. They are recognized for their consistent-ly good performance. They aren't promoted because they are perfect. In sports, the players in the starting line-up aren't there because they never make a mistake. They are there because they produce consistent results that make a positive impact on the team. Keep this in mind as you make your way toward the top.

The Key to Success is Within You

America thrives on consumerism, which operates on the underlying assumption that you, as a consumer, can find solutions to your needs and problems by purchasing a certain product, eating a specific food, taking a certain pill or paying for a particular service. Whether you are listening to the radio, watching TV, or driving down the highway, you are bombarded by advertisements that want you to believe that their product or service is the solution to your problems.

Unfortunately, this consumerist mentality perpetuates the myth that all solutions exist outside of yourself and that the power to grow, change, and improve your life is only attainable by looking elsewhere. As a society, we have surrendered and abandoned our personal power in the hope of finding solutions, wisdom, and happiness outside of ourselves. We attempt to fill personal voids, heal past hurts, and bury unresolved issues with products, food, and services. We search for answers, happiness, and peace in the marketplace. The time is now to reacquaint yourself with the power that you hold within and let go of the erroneous notion that answers, happiness, and healing can only be found outside of yourself. In order to reach your potential and attain the level of success that you are capable of, it is critical that you utilize your power of choice, consciously guide your thoughts, and focus your attention on what you want.

Regardless of whom you are or where you live, you were born with the power of choice. This power of choice is god-given and completely encompasses who you are. It is priceless, but so frequently ignored. Whether you realize it or not, you exercise the power of choice every minute of every day. You choose the thoughts you think, you choose your attitude and perspective, and you choose which actions you will take throughout the day. It is important to understand that your power of choice is weakened when you allow your emotions, your self-defeating habits, and other people's opinions drive your behavior and attitude. When you react from emotion or get stuck in a mindless "autopilot" state of mind, you are surrendering your power of choice and thereby yielding your life results. In order to harness this power of choice within yourself, it is important to be mindful and aware of each and every choice you make. Consciously make choices that are in line with your goals and in line with who you want to become.

To experience enduring success in your life, it is important that you fully utilize your power of choice and consciously guide your thoughts in positive uplifting directions. Your thoughts are the catalyst of every outcome that is created in your life. Your beliefs, feelings, habits, and results are all a reflection of your thoughts. Make the choice to think thoughts of optimism, confidence, trust, and success. If you find yourself thinking thoughts of self-doubt, fear, anxiety, or cynicism, make the choice to not buy into the negativity and deliberately change your thoughts. Exercise your power of choice.

As you utilize your power to choose and deliberately guide your thoughts in positive directions, this will allow you to focus your attention on what you want and the goals you are trying to accomplish. If your thoughts consist of fear, self-doubt, and limitation, your focus and attention will be on all the reasons why you CAN'T accomplish your goals. You will obsess about every potential challenge, every potential roadblock, and every reason why you will fail. In fact, you will convince yourself to not even try. If you exercise your power of choice and consciously make an effort to guide your thoughts in a positive, confident, and uplifting direction, you will properly focus your attention on your goals and figure out how to accomplish them. As challenges arise, you will maintain a sense of perspective, optimism, and determination and find solutions.

In summary, don't underestimate the power that you hold within yourself. The most valuable asset that you will ever own in your life, is your power to choose: the power to choose your thoughts, the power to choose your attitude, the power to choose your perspective. It has been said that on average human beings think 60,000 thoughts a day. That equates to 60,000 choices. Every day you are making thousands of choices. Out of those 60,000 choices, how many of them did you consciously choose? How many of those choices were unconscious habitual choices where you were operating on "autopilot"? Make an effort to be more mindful throughout your day. Pay attention to what choices you are making, whether they are conscious or unconscious habitual choices. It is important to understand that if you want to create different and better results in your life, you will need to start making different and better choices. When you make better choices in the thoughts that you think, the habits that you create, and the actions you take, by default, you will have your attention focused in the right direction and will create better results. Success will be yours.

Conclusion

At this point, I am confident that you have increased awareness around the differences between being a spectator and being a performer and that you better understand how each contributes to the quality of your life, your level of happiness, and level of success you experience. It is important that you get to the point where you can easily recognize when you are spectating vs. performing so that you can maintain a healthy balance. Remember, performing is all about driven or compulsive behavior and reaction. Sometimes we use performing as a distraction to feelings and emotions that we don't want to deal with. When a child is hyperactive and can't sit still, it is frowned upon, but when an adult can't sit still, we praise them for their hyperactivity and their drive for overachievement. Unfortunately, hyperactivity at any age demonstrates an imbalance in energy and doesn't allow room for pure joy, bliss, and peace. On the other hand, spectating is about stillness, observation, delayed reaction, faith, understanding, and taking control of your unique ability to contemplate, imagine, think, and make choices.

Your ability to be a spectator and observe yourself and the world is the greatest gift. It is a sacred gift we all get to experience. Being able to observe, contemplate, imagine, and make choices allows for expansion and spiritual growth. Without the ability to be a spectator, we would simply be a robot bound and gagged to our ignorance and circumstances not even aware of our successes or failures.

Before reading this book, you might not have realized how important observation, thoughts, meditation, and contemplation are as part of your efforts towards making your dreams a reality and obtaining the bliss balance. It isn't all about performing and hard work. There is a misconception in society that hard work is the only ingredient to success. The American dream is built around hard work. We are told at a young age that anything is possible as long as you work your butt off for it. We grow up thinking that successful people achieved their fame and fortune by either a stroke of luck and privilege or by hard work alone.

I would like to challenge you to change this misconception in your mind. Success, bliss, happiness, and peace don't come from only hard work and driven behavior. As I mentioned in this book, there are a lot of other factors that contribute to your level of success and happiness besides taking action. If you operate on action and performance alone, you will run yourself into the ground and never give yourself the opportunity to reach your full potential.

As you make your way through this amazing adventure we call life, keep in mind the importance of being a spectator. Remember the importance of each thought that you place your attention on. Are your thoughts in alignment with who you really are and who you aspire to be? Don't react. Use affirmations to assist you in keeping your focus in the right direction and form new beliefs about yourself and the world around you. Facilitate your spiritual growth through meditation and prayer. Develop faith in yourself, God, and all things that are good. Use your imagination and the power of visualization to create your best self and the life you want to live. Learn from your relationships. The relationships in your life provide you immediate feedback into your strengths and areas that need improvement. Be open to exploring how you are affecting your relationship dynamics. Understand the laws of the universe and how to work in alignment with them. And of course, be willing to take action. Be mindful as you take action. Work hard and work smart.

In closing, I would like to sincerely thank you for taking the time to read this book. I am grateful for the opportunity to share with you how to obtain the bliss balance - the balance of performing and spectating in order to create sustainable success, happiness, bliss, and peace. I am certain that as you apply the teachings and principles that I have discussed, your life will change for the better.

You will get closer and closer to the person that you were always meant to be, and you will experience the bliss, success, happiness, and peace that you were always meant to have.